Designing Language Teaching Tasks

Also by Keith Johnson

APPROACHES   (*with K. Morrow*)

COMMUNICATE IN WRITING

COMMUNICATE 1 AND 2   (*with K. Morrow*)

COMMUNICATION IN THE CLASSROOM   (*edited, with K. Morrow*)

THE COMMUNICATIVE APPROACH TO LANGUAGE TEACHING   (*edited, with C. J. Brumfit*)

COMMUNICATIVE SYLLABUS DESIGN AND METHODOLOGY

ENCYCLOPEDIC DICTIONARY OF APPLIED LINGUISTICS: A Handbook for Language Teaching   (*edited, with H. Johnson*)

AN INTRODUCTION TO FOREIGN LANGUAGE LEARNING AND TEACHING

LANGUAGE TEACHING AND SKILL LEARNING

NOW FOR ENGLISH 1–3

PERSPECTIVES IN COMMUNICATIVE LANGUAGE TEACHING   (*edited, with D. Porter*)

Designing Language Teaching Tasks

Keith Johnson

First published 2003 by
PALGRAVE MACMILLAN
Houndmills, Basingstoke, Hampshire RG21 6XS and
175 Fifth Avenue, New York, N.Y. 10010
Companies and representatives throughout the world

PALGRAVE MACMILLAN is the global academic imprint of the Palgrave Macmillan division of St. Martin's Press, LLC and of Palgrave Macmillan Ltd. Macmillan® is a registered trademark in the United States, United Kingdom and other countries. Palgrave is a registered trademark in the European Union and other countries.

ISBN 0–333–99047–1 hardback
ISBN 0–333–98486–2 paperback

This book is printed on paper suitable for recycling and made from fully managed and sustained forest sources.

A catalogue record for this book is available from the British Library.

Library of Congress Cataloging-in-Publication Data
Johnson, Keith, 1944–
    Designing language teaching tasks / Keith Johnson.
        p.   cm.
    Includes bibliographical references and index.
    ISBN 0–333–99047–1 (cloth) — ISBN 0–333–98486–2 (paper)
    1. Language and languages—Study and teaching.   2. Task analysis in education.   I. Title.

    P53.82 .J64 2002
    418′.0071—dc21

                                                              2002075464

10   9   8   7   6   5   4   3   2   1
12   11   10   09   08   07   06   05   04   03

Printed and bound in Great Britain by
Antony Rowe Ltd, Chippenham and Eastbourne

For Helen and Hugh

Contents

List of Figures

Acknowledgements

This book has been made possible through the generosity of the Leverhulme Trust, whose award of a Research Fellowship provided the time and resources necessary for me to analyse the data and write about it. Their generosity is much appreciated.

The data themselves were collected as part of an ESRC-funded project (entitled 'Capturing expertise in task design for instruction and assessment' – part of their Cognitive Engineering Initiative). The ESRC's role in this work is gratefully acknowledged, as is the work of the other researchers involved in that project: Jim Ridgway, Tom Ormerod, Catherine Fritz and Virginia Samuda. The opinions expressed in this book are not necessarily communal ones.

Two individuals have contributed particularly to this work. One is Virginia Samuda, who is largely responsible for the evaluative work described in Chapter 8 (and whose contribution was also made possible by the Leverhulme Trust). Virginia also provided highly useful feedback on a draft version of Chapter 8. The other person is Jayanti Banerjee who helped put the action box codes into ATLAS.ti format, and who made a number of useful suggestions regarding this coding.

I would also like to thank Keith Richards, together with an anonymous reviewer, for many insightful and useful comments on drafts of the book. My wife Helen is to be thanked for her support which has, as always, been substantial. Not the smallest part of Hugh's contribution lies in the hours when the home computer was unavailable for CD-ROM games, because Dad was using it to write.

My greatest debt is to the 16 designers who put their necks on the block, and thought aloud as they did so. They made this book, and it is about them.

1
Why Study Task Design?

1.1 Designing language teaching tasks: an expertise study and a procedural analysis

Many years ago, a colleague and I went to Italy to run a series of workshops on how to write language teaching materials for use in the classroom.[1] All the teachers attending our workshops were highly experienced, and had been selected because of their expertise as teachers. They were the *crème de la crème*. By the end of the sessions some of them had revealed themselves to be gifted materials designers, able to produce activities with accompanying teachers' notes such that the activities could be given to another teacher who would be able to use them in their own class with success. But what astonished me at the time was not how many successful materials designers emerged, but how many of the teaching *crème de la crème* showed no ability at all in the materials design realm. I think I had assumed that a good teacher would be able to produce good teaching materials for use by others. But the areas of expertise proved to be different.

This book is about designing, not whole textbooks, but one of their constituent parts – tasks or activities – for use in the foreign language classroom. Most language teaching professionals do this at some point in their careers. Some people make it their job, and become professional textbook writers. Others do it regularly but to a more modest extent. They may be senior teachers, part of whose job involves producing pieces of materials for use by teachers working on a course they are directing, or they may be teachers at any level who are in the habit of taking activities from published textbooks and modifying them for use in their particular context with their particular students.

1

The main question we are attempting to answer is: what constitutes expertise in task/activity design? We are hence undertaking an 'expertise study', attempting to identify the characteristics that single out experts from non-experts in this particular field. Expertise studies can have two components, or take two directions. One is to specify what experts are 'like'. We may, for example, end up saying that expert task/activity designers are often sensitive to the social and educational context within which their learners are working. This is an *attribute* which, we may say, experts develop and possess. The other type of statement we may end up making is to do with *procedures*. For example, we might discover that expert designers often begin by seeking real world situations in which we would use the language they wish to practise, and then try to turn one of these into a classroom task. In this book we will do attribute analysis, but there will be a concerted effort at what we shall call *procedural analysis*. We will seek to answer questions like: What do designers do first? What second? What strategies do they follow when designing a task? What issues do they confront? How do they solve them?

The intention is that this book should have something to offer a variety of readers. It aims to contribute to the research literature in what is (it is argued in the next section) a so far ignored field – the study of expertise in areas associated with language teaching. But as well as being aimed at the applied linguistic researcher, the book is also intended for all language teaching professionals. This is because it also has a practical aim, to assist language teachers both to become more proficient themselves as task designers, and also to train others to do so. To this it should be added that although the book deals with task design in the English as a foreign language area, what is said can apply equally to task design in relation to the teaching of any other foreign language.

1.2   Applied linguistic expertise studies: a sparsely populated terrain

It is surprising how little questions like those in the last paragraph but one have been asked in applied linguistics. If we consider the specific area of task/activity design, there are some books whose titles sound promising. Chief among these is Nunan's (1989) *Designing Tasks for the Communicative Classroom*. But although this book provides a useful taxonomy of language teaching tasks, it does not really make any attempt at procedural analysis. Tomlinson (1998) contains a useful section entitled 'The process of materials writing', but the amount of actual procedural analysis is small. No publication really does much more. Similarly, little attention has been paid to the study of expertise in task design. We know very little about what makes a good task designer.

If we look beyond the immediate realm of task design, yet still stay within applied linguistics and areas relevant to it, we will find more, but not an immense amount. The general educational literature field has a few studies of teacher procedures. Clark & Yinger (1987), for example, study how teachers plan their lessons and courses. Though papers like this (and there are quite a few others) do not specifically focus on the foreign language teacher, they are clearly relevant in that context. One of the few that does concentrate on language teaching is Woods's (1996) book *Teacher Cognition in Language Teaching*. This is largely an attribute (or cognition) analysis, but it does contain some useful portions of procedural analysis. There are also a number of expertise studies concerned with the language learner and the language user. This includes the good language learner studies (e.g. Naiman *et al.* 1978), and numerous studies of expertise in specific skills like reading and writing (e.g. Scardamalia & Bereiter 1991). There is also an emerging literature in the area of writing items for language tests (of which Alderson *et al.* 2000 is an example), and this area promises to develop procedural analysis in the field. So there is something in the literature relevant to applied linguistics, but not an immense amount, particularly if we think about language teaching rather than language learning and use. Chapter 2 contains brief summaries of some relevant literature.

Why is the terrain so sparsely populated? Foreign language teaching is, after all, such a common human activity – one estimate [2] has a billion people in the world today learning English (just one of the world's 4500 or so languages) as a foreign language. So one might expect quite a body of research into understanding professional expertise in language teaching. Bereiter & Scardamalia (1993) is a book we shall make much use of. In it, they argue persuasively for the importance of expertise studies in all areas. Their argument is based on the fact that the modern world is marked by great social changes which require individuals and societies to show flexibility, and a preparedness to develop new skills and areas of expertise in a comparatively short time. They in fact claim that we are on the edge of discovering a 'method of expertise' that will enable us systematically to turn novices into experts. Their argument is indeed persuasive, and suggests that there are many areas of applied linguistics which will benefit from procedural analysis and expertise studies. These include syllabus design (answering the questions: What do syllabus designers do when they design syllabuses? What makes a good syllabus designer?), teacher education, language teaching project management, and many others. An entire manifesto of expertise research suggests itself.

1.3   Tasks and activities

Apart from these arguments for research in the general fields of applied linguistics, there is also a specific reason for this kind of work in the field of task design. It is that task-based teaching is, at this present time, a topic attracting a lot of interest in language teaching. A good deal of research effort has gone into such issues as task complexity (what makes one task easier or more difficult to do) and closely observing the variables that control how learners perform when they undertake language teaching tasks. Books such as Skehan (1998) and Bygate *et al.* (2001), as well as the earlier Prabhu (1987), discuss task-based teaching at length and provide frameworks for it. Given this interest in tasks, it is timely to show an interest in how they are designed.

But it is necessary at the outset to specify how are we using the word 'task' in this book. The word may be said to have two uses, a 'specialised' and a 'general' one. In the task-based teaching literature there are, quite understandably, many attempts to define the term, and to distinguish a 'task' from an 'activity' and an 'exercise'. Figure 1.1 (based on Kumaravadivelu 1993) provides some sample definitions of the term used in this specialised, task-based-teaching related sense. The other ('general') use of the word is to mean something synonymous with 'activity', referring to 'what we give students to do in classrooms'. When many people talk about task design, they mean simply 'desiging activities for use in the class'.

Is the term task being used in its specialised or general meaning in this book? The answer is really the latter. In the study we shall be describing, we asked 16 individuals to design an activity involving the function of *describing people*. The instructions given to our subjects are on p. 29. They do not specify that the resulting activity should be a 'task' in the specialised sense of the word. In the event many designers did in fact produce activities that might be called tasks following the kinds of definition found in Figure 1.1. But some did not, and this is one reason why we cannot say the study is concerned with tasks in the specialised, task-based teaching sense. This did not worry us, and indeed we deliberately avoided asking our designers to produce tasks in line with some provided definition. One reason for this was not to

Long (1985: 89)	'a piece of work undertaken for oneself or for others, freely or for some reward'. '"Tasks" are the things people will tell you they do if you ask them and they are not applied linguists' (both p. 89)
Crookes (1986: 1)	'a piece of work or an activity, usually with a specified objective, undertaken as part of an educational course, at work, or used to elicit data for research'
Wright (1987: 48)	'instructional questions which ask, demand, or even invite learners (or teachers) to perform operations on input data'
Krahnke (1987: 57)	'the defining characteristic of task-based content is that it uses activities that the learners have to do for non-instructional purposes outside of the classroom as opportunities for language learning. Tasks are distinct from other activities to the degree that they have non-instructional purposes'
Breen (1987: 23)	'a range of workplans which have the overall purpose of facilitating language learning – from the simple and brief exercise type to more complex and lengthy activities such as group problem-solving or simulations and decision-making'
Candlin (1987: 10)	'one of a set of differentiated, sequencable, problem-posing activities involving learners' cognitive and communicative procedures applied to existing and new knowledge in the collective exploration and pursuance of foreseen or emergent goals within a social milieu'
Nunan (1989: 10)	'a piece of classroom work which involves learners in comprehending, manipulating, producing or interacting in the target language while their attention is principally focused on meaning rather than form. The task should also have a sense of completeness, being able to stand alone as a communicative act in its own right'
Swales (1990: 76)	'one of a set of differentiated, sequencable goal-directed activities drawing upon a range of cognitive and communicative procedures relatable to the acquisition of pre-genre and genre skills appropriate to a foreseen or emerging sociorhetorical situation'
Skehan (1998: 95)	'. . . a task is an activity in which: – meaning is primary – there is some communication problem to solve – there is some sort of relationship to comparable real-world activities – task completion has some priority – the assessment of the task is in terms of outcome

Figure 1.1   Some definitions of task. Based on Kumaravadivelu (1993)

prevent the participation of individuals who might be expert designers but who were either not familiar with the narrow 'task-based teaching' school of thought, or who did not subscribe to its views.

What we are, then, interested in, is how designers prepare 'activities' (or 'tasks' in the more general sense) for use in the language classroom. This statement may upset readers attracted to the book because of the word 'task' in its title, taking this to mean the book is about task-based teaching. But they should not be upset. This is because language teaching's current interest in task-based teaching can be seen as part of a more general movement over the past few decades away from an interest in the *content* of language teaching (what we teach, what our syllabus contains) towards the procedures of language teaching (how we teach, the types of activities we give our learners). This shift in focus from *what* to *how* is what is behind the development of 'communicative methodology' in the 1980s, and indeed (as a reading of Willis 1996 will reveal) many of the classroom procedures we now call tasks have much in common with what in the 1980s we called communicative activities. Task-based teaching needs to be seen in this perspective: interest in *tasks*, with all the specific characteristics mentioned in Figure 1.1, are part of a more general interest in *activities*.

We share with task-based teaching an interest in 'what we give students to do in classrooms', and we believe the study of this to be central to the concerns of a wide range of teachers. This embraces teachers who follow a task-based approach, but includes others also.

1.4   The need for applied linguistic expertise studies

But why, in practice, are expertise studies needed? How might they benefit the field? The most immediately obvious answer to these questions relates to the training of experts. If we know what constitutes expertise in an area, we will be provided with essential information on which to base the training of experts. Understanding expertise is, one might argue, the first step in training expertise. But this view introduces another important question – whether or not expertise can be taught. Can we take some of the findings of this study and turn them into lessons which will result in the creation of experts? We do not know the answer to this question, and we shall largely leave it unexplored here. We can, though, note that similar questions are being asked in other domains, and in other areas of applied linguistics. Schoenfeld (1985), for example, discusses the issue of training at some length in relation to mathematics problem solving, while in the area of language learning strategy studies, a similar question is often asked – can good learning strategies be taught? We do not yet know whether language teaching task design can be taught, but part of the rationale for studies like the one we will describe here is the possibility that it might.

This book describes work undertaken over a period of four and a half years. The first three years were taken up by a project funded by the ESRC,[3] while research in the last year and a half has been supported by the Leverhulme Trust.[4] We shall now briefly describe the outline of work done at these two stages.

1.5 The ESRC project

In 1995 the British research funding agency, the Economic and Social Research Council (ESRC), set up a programme of research in the area of cognitive engineering. The programme's website (www.cogeng.gla. ac.uk) describes cognitive engineering as modelling 'the design problems associated with interactive systems, which typically involve people, computers and organisations'. One of the projects within the programme was entitled 'Capturing expertise in task design for instruction and assessment' and it looked at two domains, the teaching of EFL and the teaching of mathematics. As this title states, the project was concerned with task design in two domains, both language and mathematics teaching. We shall here describe just the language teaching work, which had four stages.

Stage 1

Since the project dealt with tasks, we collected together a large number of language teaching tasks/activities. From this collection we chose 12 tasks that represented some major activity types (like 'information gap', 'information transfer' 'describe and draw' 'jigsaw' and so on). We printed each activity on a card (and made some other changes) in order to standardise the format. These 12 tasks were then used as input to Stage 2.

Stage 2

We were interested at this stage in what task designers 'see', on their cognitions regarding tasks, how they categorise tasks, how they evaluate various task types. We dealt with two groups of individuals. One group consisted of eight specialist designers (we shall call these S designers throughout the book). To qualify as an S designer an individual must have spent at least five years engaged in a major way in task design. All of the S designers in this study had in fact produced published sets of materials; they were textbook writers. The second group were novices in the area. They were all students following a PGCE course in modern languages teaching at St Martin's College, Lancaster. We interviewed each individual following a semi-structured format, and began by asking them to evaluate the 12 language teaching tasks we had on cards. This led to questions regarding their views on the role of tasks in language teaching. We finally asked the subjects to sort the 12 tasks into appropriate categories. Card sorting is a technique used in the psychology literature (see Chi *et al.* 1981 for example), and the way individuals group items can reveal much about how they conceptualise. One area where the technique has revealed differences is in expert/ novice comparisons, and it seemed possible that our two groups would organise the tasks on cards in different ways.[5] The 16 interviews resulting from this stage were recorded and transcribed.

Stage 3

Stage 3 involved a procedural analysis. For this study we used the same eight S designers used at Stage 2, though for various reasons it was necessary to replace the St Martin's 'novices' with a group of eight practising teachers in the process of following an MA in Linguistics for ELT course at Lancaster University. We referred to these individuals as NS (for non-specialist) designers. Later this was modified to NS/T (for non-specialist, teacher), to capture the important fact that these people, though not specialists in task design, nevertheless had much relevant experience as teachers. Seven of these NS/T designers were British native speakers of English, and one was a non-native teacher from China.

At Stage 3 our 16 subjects (8 S designers and 8 NS/T designers) were given a 'task design brief', asking them to design a task/activity which centred around the functional area of *describing people*. The design brief is given on p. 29. Wherever possible, sessions took place in the Lancaster University Psychology Department's video laboratory. Sessions usually lasted about two hours. Subjects were asked to verbalise as they designed the task. The proceedings were taped (where possible on video as well as audio tape), transcribed, coded and analysed. Because Stage 3 is what this book is mainly about, we shall describe its procedures in much more detail in subsequent chapters.

Stage 4

The final stage involved the production of a draft *Task Design Guide* intended to help anyone interested to learn how to design language teaching tasks. Part 1 of the draft guide has appeared as Samuda *et al.* (2000).[6]

The amount of data collected in the ESRC project was huge, and we found it necessary to restrict our study of it in pursuit of a few chosen aims. Attention was given to comparisons across domains, to an attempt to contribute to the problem-solving literature, and to the development of research methods for studying design. For descriptions of the project's results, see Ormerod *et al.* (1999) and Johnson (2000).

1.6 The Leverhulme project

In the ESRC study, the EFL data sets contributed to the aims as described above. But these sets are extremely rich, and provide a wealth of detailed information which goes well beyond what was utilised within the ESRC project. It was felt that if these data sets were analysed in detail they would potentially provide a full and insightful account into the specific area of foreign language teaching task design. A further aspect of the ESRC project which restricts its potential utility to the applied linguistic community is that it was taken for granted that the tasks produced by the more experienced task designers (the 'experts') were indeed superior to those produced by the 'novices'. The tasks actually produced were not subjected to any form of independent evaluation, according to agreed-on criteria.

The Leverhulme Trust provide the opportunity for the Stage 3 data to be analysed in much more detail. It also allowed a small amount of further data collection to take place. This involved providing the amount of independent evaluation mentioned above, and described in more detail in Chapter 8. This book is the result of the Leverhulme project; essentially it is based on data collected at Stage 3 of the ESRC study.

1.7 Plan of the book

In Chapter 2 we shall look in more detail at what has been done in expertise studies, both in and outside the fields of education and applied linguistics. Then, in Chapter 3, we discuss the methodology of the current study, two main issues being the use of think-aloud protocols, and matters related to coding. Chapter 4 will look at the protocols of two designers, to provide a feel for how the designers worked. Chapters 5 and 6 discuss the findings of our analysis in detail. In Chapter 7 we take from these findings what we think we can say about what makes a good task designer, and the reader who wishes to find a brief summary of conclusions will therefore find it in that chapter. In the final chapter we shall return briefly to an issue discussed above, the question of whether design expertise can be taught. We shall also look at how a group of teachers evaluated the tasks produced by our designers.

There are six appendices, and the reader may find it useful to have attention drawn at this early stage to three of them in particular. Appendix 6 contains shortened and standardised versions of the final tasks produced by all 16 of our designers, and these will be useful to refer to as contextualisation for relevant parts of discussion throughout the book. Appendix 1 contains all the codes used in analysing the protocols, and Appendix 5 collects together some pieces of 'philosophy' which our designers indulged in as they told us their thoughts.

1.8   Troublesome pronouns

In Johnson (2001a) I noted that today we are in the midst of what I called the 'great English gender crisis'. It is now no longer possible, I argued, to use 'he', 'him' and 'his' in a generic way, while alternatives like '(s)he', 'his or her' are clumsy. My solution in that book was to populate each chapter with just one gender. I shall do the same here. So in Chapter 2 all generic references (to teachers, learners, task designers and the like) are female, and in Chapter 3 they are all male, and so on through the book.

Although the present chapter uses the pronoun 'I' a lot, I have to confess to an unfashionable dislike to its use in academic discourse. I shall therefore in general resort to a distinctly unroyal 'we', which is to be understood as 'I'. When I need to refer to myself and other researchers (the more usual use of 'we'), I shall try to clarify that that is the sense.

2

Some Studies in Expertise

'One of the most exciting challenges in cognitive science today', Ericsson wrote in 1991, 'is to understand the mechanisms mediating the superior performance of experts in various domains, such as chess, physics, medicine, sport, dance, and music' (Ericsson & Smith 1991a: vii). In this chapter we shall look at how that challenge has been tackled in recent times. We begin by looking at the expertise literature in general. Then we focus on some specific areas which have particular relevance for us.

In order to keep discussion down to manageable proportions, our consideration of the literature is rather aggressively selective. There is plenty that is not discussed. This includes the work that has been done in language learning and language use strategies. It also includes much of the problem-solving literature. We shall try throughout to look forward to discussion of our own task design work in later chapters, signalling how we see the work of others to be relevant to our own.

2.1 Studies into the general nature of expertise

The study of expertise in recent times began in the 1960s with the development of artificial intelligence, and attempts to build machines capable of doing human tasks, thereby simulating areas of human expertise. In the late 1980s and early 1990s a number of books on expertise research appeared, particularly Chi *et al.* (1988), Ericsson & Smith (1991a), and Bereiter & Scardamalia (1993). We shall here describe some of the main findings in this area of research, basing our account particularly on Bereiter & Scardamalia's, who not only provide an excellent summary of the field, but also hold a view of expertise which is highly relevant to the work we shall be describing in this book.

One of the major issues in the field is whether the difference between experts and non-experts is to do with *thinking* or *knowing*. The domain where this was studied early on was playing chess. The game is traditionally considered one where 'quality of thought' is important for success. In Bereiter & Scardamalia's words (1993: 26): 'if ever there were a domain in which expertise rested on thinking abilities rather than knowledge, chess would seem to be it'. Early work in this domain was done by de Groot in the 1940s, and is described in de Groot (1978). He was interested in studying the thought processes of chess players. To do so, a number of positions from actual games were presented to different groups of subjects – grand masters, masters, experts and less skilled players. They were asked to decide what they regarded to be the 'best next move', and to think aloud as they did so. De Groot's work shatters the popular myth that chess experts, in comparison with non-experts, can think a large number of moves ahead. Far from being the case, in his study it is in fact the less skilled players who consider more possibilities than the experts. Though later research provides some counter-evidence to this finding, Bereiter & Scardamalia (1993: 28) feel safe in concluding that 'the image of the chess player as a supreme reasoner remains demolished'.

Minsky & Papert (1974) make a similar point, but with *power* and *knowledge* (rather than *thinking* and *knowledge*) as their distinction. This conceptualisation is better applicable to the machine–human comparison. We know that it is possible to produce computers with immense computational powers, capable of far outstripping humans in terms of ability to consider potential moves during a chess game. Charness (1991) reports that programmers at that time were hoping to build machines capable of searching at the rate of a billion nodes per second! Though the best of these machines can hold a challenge to grand masters, the remarkable thing is that the human experts, who lack anything like this computational power, are able to hold their own. The suggestion is that power is a poor second to knowledge.

If thinking does not play a major role in expertise, perhaps *memory* holds the key. Maybe the grand master is able to remember many more combinations of moves than the novice. De Groot's study suggests this in fact, and he finds that expert chess players are able to reproduce board configurations from memory much better than novices. Chase & Simon (1973) take this possibility forward. They find that chess experts do indeed hold in their head a large number of possible chessboard 'configurations' – patterns of around eight chess pieces that they have come across in their experience. This may lead one to believe that chess experts do indeed have exceptional memories. But when both experts and novices are given random or nonsensical configurations of pieces to memorise, the experts do no better than the novices at remembering. Hence it is not that experts have overall better memories than novices, but that they have superior memories for characteristic and meaningful patterns. Research findings in other domains, like sport and ballet dancing (Allard & Starkes 1991) as well as musical expertise, are similar. As Ericsson & Smith (1991b: 32, reporting Chase & Simon 1973) put it: 'access to aggregated past experience is the single most important factor accounting for the development of expertise'.

So expertise is something to do with *knowledge*. But what kind of knowledge? In the chess domain, knowledge of patterns or configurations seems important. Perhaps then if one were to train a novice to remember a large number of characteristic move patterns, that novice would thereby become an expert. A number of studies have looked at this possibility. Ericsson & Harris (1989), for example, found that after 50 hours of practice a subject without chess-playing experience could recall meaningful chess positions like a grand master. But it was not the case that the novice subject could play chess like a master. 'Expert knowledge', as Bereiter & Scardamalia put it (1993: 30), 'is not just a head full of facts.' It is *quality of knowledge* that is important, and in the case of chess, the crucial feature of the expert's pattern knowledge is that it should be significant and meaningful to the player. In Bereiter & Scardamalia's words again (p. 28): 'chess experts do not merely recognize thousands of chessboard patterns, they recognize them in ways that are relevant to playing the game'. Similar findings occur in another domain in which there have been many expertise studies – medical diagnosis. In experiments where specialists and non-specialists are given symptoms and asked to reach a diagnosis, it is not the case that specialists consider more symptoms than non-specialists. The difference is that specialists recognise the significant symptoms from among all those they are given, and base their judgements on those. As Kagan (1988: 485) puts it: 'the amount of clinical data obtained and the length of the decision chain appear to vary inversely with a physician's experience and level of education: more experienced physicians asking fewer questions and focusing on those likely to yield maximum information'. Bereiter & Scardamalia (1993: 58) have a phrase which captures this skill of selecting the most significant. It is a phrase which resonates much with our work in task design. The phrase is 'judgment of promisingness'; the expert knows which avenues are likely to be promising and which may turn out to be dead ends.

This characterisation of expertise correctly suggests that experts do not always go about their work in a very logical or thorough way. This can be a shock to the layperson who expects great systematicity from the expert. An anecdote will illustrate. Several years ago a friend of mine was troubled for an extended period with a bad stomach. Eventually his local doctor suggested that he should keep a daily 'diary' of what he was eating and how his stomach reacted to it. He could then take this diary with him to the appointment he had booked with a specialist for several weeks in the future. He did this, and gave the specialist the diary just before his appointment. But when he saw the specialist it soon became clear from the questions my friend was asked that the specialist had not read the diary, though he mildly denied this. My friend was baffled and hurt by this. Presumably what the specialist was doing was to exercise his own judgement of promisingness to the symptoms. He had no need to read a lengthy and tedious account of my friend's eating habits and their results.

Another domain where there are compatible findings is the field of general problem solving, where work has been done on the different problem-solving strategies of experts and novices. Newell & Simon's (1972) celebrated work in this field shows that a successful problem-solving strategy is the one called 'means–end analysis'. In this you work 'backwards' from the final state required, and develop stages whereby that final state can be reached. This strategy is successful, but it is also hard work, and requires a lot of effortful thinking. A far simpler strategy may be to work 'forward', starting with what you are given and trying to move from that towards what is required. This is not such hard work, but it does rely on being able to interpret what you are given, and recognising what is significant in it. Work in the medical diagnosis domain (Patel & Groen 1991) suggests that novices, who do not have the store of 'significant symptom patterns' that experience provides, will often follow the more effortful 'means–end' analysis procedure. Specialists, on the other hand, are likely to use their store of significant symptom patterns to short circuit the procedure. This indeed fits in with the findings (Hunt 1989) that novices often start with a diagnosis and see whether the symptoms they are confronted with fit in with the diagnosis, while the specialist will move from symptoms to diagnosis.

Findings like these, when considered together with the general view that knowledge is more important than thinking, seem to lead us towards a curious conclusion – that experts may often work *less* hard than novices. It is the novice who does the hard thinking, while the expert uses a series of short cuts to avoid the hard work and arrive at the solution by the quickest possible route. Important in understanding this point (which is central to Bereiter & Scardamalia's views) is the realisation that the behaviour of both novices and experts, in the diagnosis studies for example, is entirely logical and natural. Thus the novices are undertaking the difficult means–end analysis because they are unequipped for the simpler method the experts tend to use. Similarly, the experts will use the simpler method because it is available to them. Those who have knowledge do not need to think so much, while those lacking the knowledge base are forced into the harder route. Each is making the best out of what is at her disposal.

But what would an expert diagnostician do if she were faced with a real problem that lay outside her experience, and for which she did not have a set of significant symptom patterns to hand? This question raises a problem, Bereiter & Scardamalia note, with the many expert–novice studies in the literature. Such studies characteristically take a group of experts and one of novices, and give them the same task to undertake (solving a chess problem or working out a medical diagnosis, whatever it be). The task must be the same for the two groups so that their performance and behaviour can be compared. The task has to be 'simple' enough for the novices to tackle, and an unfortunate consequence of this is that the task is likely to be well within the capacities of the experts, not nearly taxing them to the full. In such circumstances the amount of effort the experts have to put into the task is indeed likely to be less than that of the novices. It may also be that different strategies are followed by the two groups, with (for example) novices using more means–end analysis than experts. But if the task is easy for one group and a challenge to the other group, comparisons arising out of it are unfair, and findings based on it are unsafe. We need experimental situations where experts too are taxed. Bereiter & Scardamalia argue that a study by Joseph & Patel (1986) provides just such a situation. In it, the experts too have to put much effort into the solution, and may certainly become involved in means–end analysis.

Expert–novice studies are therefore likely to reach findings suggesting effortless performance on the part of experts. Such findings do have a degree of intuitive attraction; we think for example of the expert singer who appears to be hitting difficult notes without effort, or the tennis champion who manages to make the game look like child's play. But we also recognise intuitively that the apparent ease of experts often belies immense effort, and this is the picture Bereiter & Scardamalia wish to paint. 'Many experts we know', they say (1993: 34), 'are active striving people. They work long hours… and they tend to set standards for themselves and others that are always at least slightly beyond reach.' Bereiter & Scardamalia illustrate this from their own field of study – writing. Work in this field seems to offer a solution to the research problem of providing a task which will tax both novices and experts alike. Subjects can be asked to write an essay on a topic capable of either complex or simple treatment. When that is the situation, Bereiter & Scardamalia's evidence is that the experts are the ones who put more work into the task. In the study reported in Scardamalia & Bereiter (1991) for example, experts plan their writing more, take more time to start (write the first sentence, that is), agonise more over the correct choice of words, make more false starts. Novices are faster, more fluent… and often put down the first thing that comes into their heads. It may be that our particular domain, language teaching task design, is also one that can provide tasks which challenge novices and experts alike. If so, and if Bereiter & Scardamalia are right, we might expect the experts consistently to put more work into the activity than novices. Or will we, on the other hand, find evidence in our experts of what Simon (1981) calls 'satisficing' behaviour? This is where an individual does the minimum amount of work to get the task done.

The phenomenon of satisficing raises the thorny issue of how we recognise what an expert is. Traditional expert–novice studies select their experts using 'external' or 'social' criteria. An expert by these criteria would be someone generally recognised in society as surpassing in a particular sphere. The criteria are likely to place importance on length of experience. So a diagnostician who has spent 20 years at her work might be regarded as an expert. But we all know of people who, despite a huge amount of experience, have not really become expert. Woods (1996: 270) reminds us of the adage that one teacher may have had ten years of experience, while another may have had one year's experience ten times. Bereiter & Scardamalia handle this phenomenon by distinguishing between *expert* and *experienced non-expert*. We need to be sure, they argue, that our training programmes produce the former rather than the latter; if all we provide is practice in the relevant skill, we are unlikely to succeed in this. Practice will produce experience, but not necessarily expertise.

It seems unlikely that studies of expertise will be able to do entirely without reference to external or social criteria. Certainly Scardamalia & Bereiter's (1991) study of writing expertise talks about 'professional writers' and well-known journalists. De Groot too uses a kind of 'social' definition of chess expertise when he identifies groups of 'grand masters' and 'masters'. But, it is argued in Ericsson & Smith (1991b), we should support such criteria with performance-related measures. We need to be able to identify a task which truly encapsulates expertise in a particular domain. We then need to identify who performs the task well, and who not. As we have seen, in chess de Groot (1978) asks subjects to identify the best next move in a middle-game position, and this task is felt to involve characteristics important to chess in general. The task design activity we give our subjects (see p. 29) is our attempt at such a measure. But note that our initial identification of experts has followed an external social criterion. Hence we recognise as an S designer (expert) someone who has been designing tasks full time for a period of five years. If our study is to avoid the criticism that we fail to distinguish expert and experienced non-expert, we need to have some measure of how our subjects perform on the task design activity we give them. We discuss this further in Chapter 8.

2.2 Specific expertise studies of particular relevance

2.2.1 Mathematical problem solving: Schoenfeld (1985)

Another area which, like chess, can be considered a 'high-order thinking skill' is mathematical problem solving. This area has not received anything like the attention paid to chess. But one book, Schoenfeld (1985), is in his own words 'about doing, understanding, and teaching mathematical problem solving' (p. 1). Though the domain (mathematics) is quite different from our own (language teaching), there are two aspects of Schoenfeld's study that make it particularly relevant for us. One is that he is indeed dealing with a 'high-order thinking skill', and he himself expresses the view (p. xii) that what he has to say will be relevant to the study of other such skills, which may be said to include task design. Secondly, Schoenfeld is concerned above all with *process* – what individuals actually do when they solve mathematical problems. This preoccupation with process is one that we share.

The book is divided into two parts. In the first, Schoenfeld outlines the model which he has developed for the analysis of mathematical problem-solving behaviour. In Part 2 he describes a number of studies intended to provide empirical support for the model. Because the two parts cover the same ground – first in 'theory' then in 'practice' – we shall here treat them together, focusing selectively on those issues likely to be most relevant to our own work.

Schoenfeld's model identifies four components which need to be described if mathematical problem-solving behaviour is to be understood.

These he labels as *resources, heuristics, control,* and *belief systems*. We shall look at each in turn.

Resources

'In order to understand what someone does while working', Schoenfeld says, 'we need to have an inventory of what the individual knows, believes, or suspects to be true' (p. 17). He lists the different kinds of resources the problem solver requires. Domain knowledge (knowledge of mathematics in this case) is naturally on the list. But this is just one of what Schoenfeld calls 'a spectrum of relevant competencies'. As we have seen elsewhere in this chapter, it is not the possession of domain knowledge itself that is important, despite the fact that expertise is often described in just these terms (knowing a lot about your subject area). What counts is what the individual does with that knowledge. Schoenfeld's list of relevant competencies therefore includes the ability to perform problem-solving procedures. An example of the kind of resource Schoenfeld includes is the ability to associate a problem with a problem type: 'the individual recognizes the particular situation as being of a specific type (say type X) and immediately thinks of the techniques relevant for dealing with type X situations' (p. 50). This is called 'having a type X schema'.

A good part of Schoenfeld's discussion of resources is concerned with the way in which knowledge is conceptualised by experts – the kinds of information structures that they hold. This is the sort of information we were concerned with at Stage 2 of the ESRC project, described in Chapter 1.

Heuristics

In the Preface to his book, Schoenfeld acknowledges a debt to an early writer on problem solving, George Pólya, and his 1945 book *How To Solve It*. Pólya defines heuristics as 'mental operations typically useful for the solution of problems'. Some examples of the heuristics Schoenfeld identifies are given in Figure 2.1. The heuristics exemplified in the figure differ considerably in their scope. 'Working forward from data' and 'working backwards' are the very general overall problem-solving strategies discussed earlier in this chapter. One might expect others of Schoenfeld's example heuristics (like 'drawing figures') to have less general application.

Pólya (1945) provides an overall framework for the stages subjects go through in the course of solving a problem like a mathematical puzzle. This sequence is shown in Figure 2.2.

- Exploiting analogies
- Introducing auxiliary elements in a problem or working auxiliary problems
- Arguing by contradiction
- Working forward from data
- Decomposing and recombining
- Exploiting related problems
- Drawing figures
- Specialising
- Using *reductio ad absurdum* and indirect proof
- Varying the problem
- Working backwards

Figure 2.1 Some examples of heuristics, modified from Schoenfeld (1985: 23)

Understanding the problem

↓

Devising a plan

↓

Carrying out the plan

↓

Looking back

Figure 2.2 Pólya's problem-solving stages (as reported in Schoenfeld 1985: 24)

In the empirical part of his book (Part 2, Chapter 9), Schoenfeld describes a number of verbal protocols of subjects thinking aloud while attempting to solve a mathematical problem. In his analysis of these protocols, Schoenfeld elaborates on Pólya's framework. The result is a framework involving six episode types: *reading, analysis, exploration, planning, implementation, verification* (to which is added a further category called *transition*, being the movement from one episode type to another).

It is natural that we shall also be greatly concerned with the identification of heuristics. The overall sequencing of episodes during task design is also an issue we address, and the framework we adopt (discussed in Chapter 3) owes much to both Pólya and Schoenfeld.

Control

In his discussion of heuristics, Schoenfeld makes the point (p. 73) that at any given moment in problem solving, the number of heuristic choices available to the problem solver may be huge. The expert is able to select the most potentially useful and relevant heuristics from the large choice available. Her choice is made by the use of control strategies of monitoring and overseeing. The same point was made earlier in relation to symptoms in medical diagnosis – expertise lies in the ability to select meaningfully from the totality of symptoms displayed. Bereiter & Scardamalia's phrase 'judgment of promisingness' comes to mind again.

Schoenfeld argues at length that control plays a very important role in mathematical problem solving. He illustrates the importance of control skills by considering the protocol of one expert problem solver who does not possess great domain knowledge related to the problem being tackled, yet managed to solve it. 'Largely through efficient work at the control level,' Schoenfeld says, 'the problem-solver marshalled his cognitive resources' and was able to find the answer. The protocol shows that 'a monitor-assessor-manager was always close at hand during the solution attempt. Rarely did more than a minute pass without there being some clear indication that the entire solution process was being watched and controlled, both at local and global levels' (p. 310).

Schoenfeld notes that different terms are used in different fields for what he is calling control. In artificial intelligence studies one speaks of 'executive decisions', in business of 'managerial decisions', in the military field of 'strategic' (as opposed to tactical) decisions, and in psychology of 'metacognition'.[1] In some of these fields, research has given similar importance to control skills and, as Goh (1998) notes, there is a huge amount of literature on the value of metacognition (control) in learning in general. One might well imagine that control skills are as important to task design as to mathematical problem solving, that good task designers will possess them, and that these will be evidenced in their design protocols.

The empirical part of Schoenfeld's book discusses at length the types of control mechanisms he finds in the protocols he analyses. He lists five types of 'managerial behaviours', and these are shown in Figure 2.3. In our own study we shall seek evidence of similar managerial behaviours. But we need to approach the issue with caution. In relation to one of his managerial behaviours, Schoenfeld makes the point that 'assessment is not always desirable or appropriate. In a schema-driven solution [one, that is, taken from the problem solver's repertoire], for example, one should simply implement the solution without assessment unless or until something untoward happens. A simple-minded model that simply checks for assessments at a series of previously designated places (such as transition points between episodes....) would

- Selecting perspectives and frameworks for working a problem
- Deciding at branch points which direction a solution should take
- Deciding in the light of new information whether a path already embarked upon should be abandoned
- Deciding what should be salvaged from something abandoned, or adopted from approaches considered but not taken on wholesale
- Monitoring and assessing implementation 'on line', and looking for signs that executive intervention might be appropriate

Figure 2.3 Schoenfeld's managerial behaviours (1985: 295)

miss the point entirely' (p. 315). The point is a manifestation of one made earlier in this chapter: that experts often do not go about their work in a thorough or 'logical' manner. They are often able to take short cuts, and this may mean that control skills may not in fact 'be evidenced in their design protocols' (the prediction we made earlier). Indeed, it is not too far fetched to imagine that novices, with their lack of relevant knowledge, may show more evidence of management than the experts. The issue needs to be explored empirically in some detail.

Belief systems

In his discussion of belief systems, Schoenfeld explores the views held by his subjects, particularly the novices, regarding the roles of knowledge and thought in mathematical problem solving. He observes a widespread belief that formal mathematics has nothing to do with problem solving. This leads subjects, even those with good mathematical knowledge, not to employ that knowledge in problem solving. Instead they resort to a kind of 'naïve thinking', using common sense to work out the solution. He also observes that many novice subjects do not use thinking as a discovery tool to move them logically towards an answer. Instead they put effort into trying to retrieve a solution from memory. The second of these findings in particular resonates with what occurs in task design. Many designers, experts and non-experts alike, devote much energy to finding suitable tasks in their already existing repertoire, and modifying these for the *describing people* function. We discuss this in Chapter 6.

The empirical part of Schoenfeld's book contains detailed discussion on an issue highly relevant to our concerns. This is the question of research methodology, related to the collection of data through think-aloud protocols, and the coding of such data. We shall refer to Schoenfeld's discussion in our Chapter 3.

2.2.2   Teacher cognition and behaviour

In the general educational literature there are a number of studies dealing with teacher cognition and behaviour. Interest in this area has grown steadily since the early 1970s, and there have been three major foci of attention: the cognitive processes underlying teacher judgements and decisions, teacher planning (of courses and lessons), and the interactive judgements and decisions of teachers (interactive because they take place in class while in interaction with learners).

The teacher planning area is of particular interest to us, and an overview of research in that field is found in Clark & Yinger (1987), on whom some of the following is based. A major finding has been that teachers do not follow the 'rules' for planning they are likely to have been taught at training college. These rules are described in Tyler (1950). The prescribed planning algorithm has four steps, to be followed in order – first, specify objectives; second, select learning activities; third, organise learning activities; and fourth, specify evaluation procedures. In an early large-scale study, Taylor (1970) looked at how teachers planned their courses in three domains: English, science and geography. The finding was that teachers did not follow this algorithm at all. Other researchers since have found the same. This element of teacher 'rebelliousness' (not doing what they have been trained to do) is interesting to us because it may have a parallel in task design behaviour. There is no one generally accepted algorithm for task design, as there seems to have been for teacher planning. But we discuss in Chapter 5 the way that many designers do not follow the design procedures that they themselves seem to perceive as being the right way of going about the activity.

What then does the rebellious teacher do? Taylor (1970) finds that teachers start their planning by thinking about contextual factors (who the learners are, what time and resources are available and so on), then look at learning situations (types of situations likely to interest the learners), then purposes (the aims of the course). Other researchers reach similar conclusions. Peterson *et al.* (1978) record 12 teachers thinking aloud as they plan a series of lessons. They find that most planning time is spent on content, then instructional processes. The least amount of time is dedicated to objectives. Planning lessons is likely to have something in common with planning/devising tasks, and for this reason such findings are of interest; it will be important for us to consider what the preoccupations of task designers are as they prepare activities for classroom use.

Clark & Yinger (1979) is another paper which reaches conclusions of potential relevance to us. They study five teachers preparing lessons.

Content	'the subject matter to be taught'
Materials	'those things that children can observe and/or manipulate'
Activity	'the thing the teacher and student will be doing during the lesson'
Goals	'the teachers' general aim for the task'
Student	'especially his abilities, needs and interests'
Social cultural context	'the class as a whole and its sense of "groupness"'

Figure 2.4 Task elements, as described in Shavelson & Stern (1981: 478)

One of their findings is that the planning is not linear but cyclical, moving from general idea to detailed plan through series of elaborations. In Chapter 6 we consider the evidence for a cyclical strategy in task design. Clark & Yinger also found planning styles differing from individual to individual. The question of individual variation in design style is also important to anyone concerned with training task designers. This is an issue we briefly touch on in Chapter 8. Trainers will need to take differing design styles into account, and not attempt to force one monolithic strategy on to all potential designers.

There are a number of studies in the field (including Clark & Yinger 1979, Yinger 1977 and Zahorik 1975) which suggest that teachers use the 'instructional activity' as their unit of planning. This is a finding that strengthens our claim that it is important to study the way activities are designed. In their valuable summary of research in the area, Shavelson & Stern (1981: 477) propose using the word 'task' rather than 'activity' in this context (because 'activity' is used in other senses in the literature). They provide an overview of how different studies have divided the notion of task into a number of elements. These are shown in Figure 2.4. If we are to come to grips with the details of task design, identifying the 'elements of a task' must clearly be a major concern of our research. In Chapter 3 we describe the codes developed to classify task elements.

One book of particular relevance to our work is Woods (1996). He reports on a study which looks over an extended period of time at eight ESL teachers working in various university settings in east-central Canada. He is interested in the way his subjects plan their courses and convert their plans into actual lessons. He is also concerned with 'how information about teaching, learning and language is related to the actions and events that the students face in the classroom' (1996: 24). Data for the study were collected by means of interviews, observations and introspection based on videos of teaching.

The most obvious relevance of this work to us is that it is one of the very few studies concerned with the domain of foreign/second language teaching. But there are other points of contact with our work, and indeed with Schoenfeld's. One is that Woods is describing a large-scale activity. In his opening chapter Woods makes the point that he is dealing with events that occur within the structure of entire lessons or episodes. He notes that much of the literature has been concerned with micro levels, mapping local movements in classroom behaviour. Sinclair & Coulthard's (1975) small-scale sequences of *teacher initiate student → respond → teacher evaluate* are an example. A similar point is made by Schoenfeld who says: 'to my knowledge there have not been formally defined schemes for analysing protocol data at the macro-scopic (or strategic) level' (1985: 286). It is therefore necessary for both Woods and Schoenfeld to develop schemes of analysis that have macro as well as micro levels, and to show how the former fit within the latter. Woods's framework has *global conceptual units, intermediate conceptual units* and *local conceptual units*. We require a similar framework, and our own solution is described in Chapter 3.

A further point of contact is that Woods (again like Schoenfeld) is dealing with highly complex data, not amenable to simple analysis. He emphasises this on a number of occasions. At one point (1996: 110), for example, he notes that one event may fall into a number of hierarchies, fulfilling more than one function at the same time. He uses Anderson's (1983) notion of 'tangled hierarchies' to deal with this aspect of the data. There are other phrases in the literature which express the com-plexity of data based on protocols of high-level thought patterns. Kagan (1988) uses the phrase 'ill-structured problems' (from Reitman 1965) to describe medical diagnostic procedures, and the term well fits task design too. Perhaps the most descriptive term of all is Ackoff's (1979, cited in Clark & Yinger 1987: 97). He finds similarities between the thought patterns of teachers and managers: 'managers', he says, 'are not confronted with problems that are independent of each other, but with dynamic situations that consist of complex systems of changing prob-lems that interact with each other. I call such situations *messes*.' Task design procedures are often 'messes', and again it is in Chapter 3 that we will consider how they can be analysed to capture the complexity (and sometimes the inelegance) of the procedures.

Woods, again like Schoenfeld and ourselves, is concerned with process and not just product. In the course of his study he identifies a number of planning procedures, and these are discussed in relation to the three main points at which planning is undertaken: before the course begins, before individual lessons and during lessons. Examples of his planning procedures are (with his definitions given in brackets, from Woods 1996: 146): *generating* ('expanding the resources that can be used within the current constraints'), *weighing and selecting* ('tentatively choosing, or giving positive weighting to specific units') and *mapping* ('adapting conceptual structure to fit into scheduled time slots and deciding what will be done in what periods of time').

Woods makes other points in relation to processes that, we have noted, have been made elsewhere in the literature. Like others working on teacher planning, he finds that teachers do not follow the elegant planning models taught at training colleges. He also follows other writers on expertise, including Schoenfeld, in distinguishing between subject (domain) knowledge and other important types of knowledge. In Schoenfeld one of these types of knowledge is to do with problem-solving ability, and in Woods's case it is what he calls 'lesson structure knowledge'. Woods recognises that the expert teacher planning her lessons uses not just subject matter knowledge but also an understanding of how lessons are structured.

2.2.3 Decomposition strategies and opportunistic planning

There is discussion in the design and problem-solving literatures on what are sometimes described as decomposition strategies – how designers and problem solvers break down tasks in order to produce designs or solutions. The two common decomposition strategies are known as breadth-first (BF) and depth-first (DF). In the BF strategy, the designer identifies a number of possible solutions, and briefly explores these before committing herself to developing any one solution in depth. The advantage of this strategy is that it avoids premature commitment to a final solution that may, following later detailed examination, have to be abandoned. Potential solutions can be dropped without massive amounts of work being lost. But there is also an accompanying disadvantage. The strategy is heavy on cognitive load; the designer has to keep several possible solutions in mind – constantly evaluating them against each other – before a final choice is made. The DF strategy involves exploring one solution in depth from an early stage. The advantage is lightness of cognitive load, but there is the concomitant danger of commitment to one solution which might eventually prove itself inappropriate and have to be abandoned late in the day.

In a paper describing part of the project being discussed here, Ormerod *et al.* (1999) cite examples of the view that BF is associated with experts, DF with novices. Perez *et al.* (1995), for example, describe experts and novices who were preparing lesson plans for teaching students to trouble-shoot a diesel engine simulator. They found that experts showed greater adherence to BF principles than novices, who typically designed in a DF manner. But there are others who find that experts use a mixture of DF and BF, and some (particularly Ball & Ormerod 1995) are of the opinion that such a mixture will be optimal. Among the reasons why an entirely BF strategy may be avoided are purely practical ones, such as that those overseeing the design process may become dissatisfied if too much time is spent looking at hypothetical alternatives, before evidence of in-depth planning (and 'progress') is provided. In Chapter 6 we shall consider how our designers behave in relation to the BF and DF strategies.

A further area relevant to our study relates to the notion of *opportunistic planning*, discussed particularly in Hayes-Roth & Hayes-Roth (1979). They note that the generally accepted model of planning is a top-down one. The top-down planner begins by making high-level decisions which are broken down into sub-goals. Each of these sub-goals is then executed in order of priority. But in reality, Hayes-Roth & Hayes-Roth note, some planners follow a less neat and coherent pathway; indeed it is one which on occasions 'might appear chaotic' (p. 276). Hayes-Roth & Hayes-Roth investigate this less systematic approach by means of an 'errand-planning task' which they give to a number of subjects who are asked to think aloud as they tackle it. The subjects are given a list of 'errands' which need to be done on a particular day, including such items as 'pick up medicine for your dog from the vet', and 'meet a friend for lunch at one of the restaurants'. The list is a long one and contains more errands than can be done in the time available. The subjects therefore have to prioritise, deciding which errands are the most important. Subjects are also given a map of the hypothetical town showing the relevant locations of shops, restaurants, etc.

Hayes-Roth & Hayes-Roth describe the protocol of one typical subject. He begins by defining his goals, deciding which errands are important and which less so. But when he comes to plan the order in which he will do the jobs, he does not follow a strict order of importance. Instead he identifies areas of town, and does all the errands in that area while he is in the vicinity. In Hayes-Roth & Hayes-Roth's words, 'he decides to treat the errands in the southeast corner as a cluster. He plans to go to the southeast corner and do those errands at about the same time' (p. 282). Hayes-Roth & Hayes-Roth describe such planning as 'opportunistic', and the planning model they produce is developed to take such opportunistic behaviour into account. We shall find some examples of opportunistic planning on the part of our task designers.

2.3   Conclusion

Studies of the sort reported in this chapter provide useful guidance as to what we might look for in our own study. They offer a ready-made set of 'judgments of promisingness' as to which directions it will be useful for us to look in. They also provide guidance as regards research methodology. On a general level the studies all deal with the same research problem – how to reveal and analyse high-level thought processes as they occur in relation to some procedure. The next chapter will focus on research methodology, and will consider how approaches to this general type of research problem can be applied to the specific domain of task design.

3
Studying Task Designers at Work

'Ill-defined problems', 'tangled hierarchies' and 'messes'. These are all phrases we suggested in Chapter 2 might be used to describe activities such as language-teaching task design. How can such an ill-defined, tangled, messy phenomenon be studied? This chapter is devoted to the research methodology we used in the study. There are four broad areas we shall cover. The first relates to the design brief we gave our subjects, which they were expected to follow in the design of their task. The second concerns the think-aloud protocols we used to collect data. Thirdly, we look at alternative ways there might have been of collecting data. In the final section we consider how the data, once collected, were coded.

3.1 The design brief

We wanted our subjects to design tasks which were comparable with each other, so that the two groups (S and NS/T designers) could be compared, as well as making comparisons between individuals possible. Figure 3.1 is the design brief (Cohen & Hosenfeld 1981 would call it the 'elicitation format') we finally arrived at, after a number of false starts.

The development of this brief raised a number of issues to do with *how much* guidance we should give to our subjects, and *what type* of guidance it should be. Underlying the question of *how much* are a set of opposing arguments. On the one hand we want our subjects to have the freedom to design tasks that fit in with their views about language teaching and reflect their own design style (a factor one might call 'designer proclivity'). We also want them to develop tasks for the types of learners and contexts they are familiar with, reflecting in other words their 'designer experience'. These factors can argue in favour of a less detailed specification, one that perhaps does not state the exact nature

Designers were given a piece of paper carrying the following instructions for task design. They were asked to read the brief out aloud before starting their design.

You are asked to imagine that you have been teaching, or writing materials for, an adult monolingual group of learners at intermediate level. The group is studying a general English course in their own country. They meet for a two-hour class once a week. There are approximately 15–20 learners in the class.

In recent lessons you have been dealing with the general functional area of describing people. This has included coverage of simple descriptive statements of the He/she is very tall/short sort, but also more complex descriptions of character as well as physical appearance.

You now wish to give your learners a 'communicative' activity to practise this area further. You want the learners to interact as much as possible, with as many different members of the class as possible involved. Although reading and writing may be involved, you are most concerned to provide opportunities for speaking skills. You want the activity to last roughly between 15 and 30 minutes.

The materials you produce are to be used in the next day or so, and your activity needs to be worked out in sufficient detail for this to happen. This should include preparation of any worksheets. It would also be useful for us if you were to prepare clear written instructions on how to use the activity. If you are a teacher, you might imagine these instructions to be for a colleague who is to teach the activity. If you are a materials writer, the instructions might take the form of Teachers' Notes.

Figure 3.1 The design brief given to subjects

of the task required or the teaching context it is intended for. In this way, designers would be given as much freedom as possible to develop tasks in line with their proclivities and experience.

Standing against this is our need for comparative information. We must be able to compare the procedures of individual designers, and to make comparisons between the major groups – our S and NS/T designers. The more we can specify the nature of the task we require, and the context for which it should be designed, the more we can expect comparability. A further argument for detailed specification is that we need to provide subjects with a certain amount of information to make design possible. Many course designers write with more specific contextual information than we provide and, one might argue, a good degree of such information is necessary if satisfactory tasks are to result. It is certainly the case that many of our designers are unhappy with what the design brief does *not* tell them, and this is particularly true of the NS/T group.

Although we say above that many course designers write with more specific contextual information than we provide in the brief, it is also true that many designers work with much less such information. Professional materials writers (the category most of our S designers fall into) are often not provided with much contextual information at all, particularly if they are writing for a global audience, in other words for learners working in a great diversity of contexts. We may wish to argue strongly that the production of global materials is a bad practice best abolished. But it remains the state of affairs that exists, and part of expertise in materials production is to be able to do it.

The contrary forces we have just described – for *less* and *more* specification – pull in opposite directions, and the brief in Figure 3.1 is our attempt to balance them. These forces can also be seen at play when we consider *what type* of specification it is appropriate to provide. The nature of the activity required is one aspect of this. We have chosen a functional area (*describing people*) for our task. Language pedagogy based on the teaching of what Wilkins (1972) called 'categories of communicative function' (of which *describing people* is an example) was particularly popular in the 1970s and early 1980s. But it was subject to a number of criticisms in the 1980s (see Brumfit 1981 for example), and although textbooks written today often have a functional dimension, they are rarely if ever organised completely in functional terms.

We can expect any group of language teaching task designers, brought together for whatever purpose, to have very differing views on functional teaching. Some will regard it with enthusiasm, embrace it, and have had plenty of experience with it. Others may have strong (and entirely cogent) objections to functional materials and little experience at their design. Widely differing proclivities and experience were in fact what we found. Two or three of our S designers had had considerable experience in functional materials development and were clearly comfortable with it. Others not so. Here is D1 soon after reading the brief aloud:

> *I do have a bit of a problem with this kind of activity of describing people because although it is the sort of thing which is very popular amongst materials writers and so on and teachers, when you think about real life there aren't that many times when you actually go about producing some sort of long description of people.*
>
> (D1)

And here is the first comment another designer makes after looking through the brief:

> *OK so I have to, I have to produce something which I probably normally wouldn't do.*
>
> (D4)

Given these differing proclivities and experiences, are we not being unfair to some designers by setting up the brief in this way? Those who dislike functional materials, or are inexperienced with them, will surely be at a disadvantage, and are likely to produce inferior materials. The implication of this view is that we should have given designers more freedom to develop activities more in terms of their proclivities and experience.

Similar points may be made about other aspects of the specification. As we have seen, some designers want more contextual information than we provide. Nevertheless, some contextual information is given. It is specified, for example, that the learners are monolingual, studying in their own country, adults and intermediates. But among our subjects there will be designers who have had little experience of such learners. Some may never have taught a monolingual group in their own country, while others may not have experience with adult intermediates. Again, these designers are likely to be at a disadvantage in the task design activity, and again the suggestion is that we should provide more designer freedom by being less prescriptive about our requirements.

The major counterargument against more designer freedom and less prescription remains the necessity to impose some standardisation on the output of our various designers, so that comparison is possible. But there are two further arguments to suggest that detailed specification should not be too harmful. One argument says that experts should have the flexibility to design in situations they are not familiar with. There is some support for this in the skill psychology literature. Legge & Barber (1976) retell a story, taken from Johnson (1961), where the moral is that versatility is indeed a hallmark of skilled behaviour. It is the story of the 'Wood Choppers' Ball'. This is about a contest between two woodsmen, both highly skilled with the axe. On a large number of tests they come out as equal, and the judge has the problem of distinguishing them. Eventually it is decreed that they should swap axes, and chop with each other's axes, rather than the ones they are used to. The champion emerges as the one who can adapt better to using an unfamiliar axe.[1]

The second argument is that being asked to produce a task which fits in neither with one's proclivities nor one's experience is common in real-world task design. It is likely that at some point in his career, every 'anti-functionalist' is going to be asked to produce a piece of functional material. It is even more likely that a task designer will be asked to produce materials for an audience he has little experience with. This is not of course an ideal state of affairs. But it is one that exists, and one might claim that expertise in task design involves being able to show the flexibility to design outside one's proclivities and experience.

It is in fact the case that several of the S designers who grumbled at the nature of the task they were asked to design, then get on with it and produce good tasks. But the counterarguments we give above are only half the story. Although we might expect flexibility from our expert designers, the fact remains that a pro-functionalist with experience at teaching monolingual adult intermediates in their own country has the advantage. He is being asked to chop with his own axe. The teacher whose proclivities and experience lie elsewhere is being made to chop with an unfamiliar axe.

A further possible criticism is that the brief (and behind it the entire study we are describing) is not sufficiently specific in terms of the type of task required. Something more clearly a 'task' in the senses found in Chapter 1 would be required. We have already agued against this position in Chapter 1, stating that we do not wish this work to be associated too strongly with any one view of language teaching. To take the argument a step further: we might claim that expertise in task design will have the same elements whatever tradition the designer is working in. So good 'task-based' designers, good 'communicative' designers, good 'audio-lingual' designers will share much in common. They are all good designers, who happen to be working in different traditions.

Why do we ask our subjects to provide such detail, with worksheets, instructions and teachers' notes? Our experience has been that there are many teachers who can produce good general ideas – sketches for interesting tasks – but who fall down when they try to construct the details. In task design it is our belief that a good many devils lie in the detail, and we wanted to be sure the designers were forced into the stage of detailed planning.

Given all these issues concerning the nature and extent of the design brief specification, one might well ask whether the activity we gave our subjects was regarded as an authentic one, having face validity for designers. Does our design activity capture the processes designers actually follow? With hindsight it would have been useful to ask all designers this question at the end of the design sessions. In the event only a few were asked, and although no firm conclusions can be drawn from the responses, they did in general affirm that the process they had gone through was realistic. Here is one exchange that exemplifies this:

Int: ...*how much like the way work you actually design do you think some of your thinking process and your designing process were? Was it at all similar or was it just something completely different from what you usually do?*

D7:   No I think it's very similar, it's very similar, because I started out by trying to, you know to get hold of the context as much as I could from the piece of paper and to see what the task required as it were in terms of length and numbers of people involved yeh and then start from there and see then what is possible. So, no I, as far as I know because I can't say that I've ever sort of consciously reflected on the task design process before but what I was doing here you know didn't seem to me totally dissimilar you know from what I have done when writing the material for a course book. It seems, no it seems very similar.

3.2   Concurrent verbalisation

3.2.1   Introspection and verbal reports

The technique we use to collect data involves asking our subjects to think aloud as they design a task. This is called concurrent verbalisation and it is one of a number of techniques which involve introspection. Introspection, where subjects reflect on their own thoughts and mental processes, has had a very chequered history in psychology. One of the pioneers of introspection was the German psychologist Wilhelm Wundt, born in 1832. For him, psychology was the study of living systems from 'within themselves', and this almost by definition involved self observation. Wundt also believed that psychology should be conducted through rigorously controlled experimentation. Systematic and highly detailed methods of introspection were therefore developed, and based on these a school of psychology emerged which was known as 'introspectionism'. Somewhat ironically – because the technique was often intended to reveal processes that were spontaneous – the subjects were highly trained to introspect. The school became discredited by the early behaviourist psychologists, who saw no place for mental reflection as a reliable means of collecting data. Since that time behaviourism has itself suffered a degree of discredit, and introspection has enjoyed something of a revival. Newell & Simon (1972) used introspective techniques in their study of human problem solving, and are credited with the term 'protocol analysis'. A protocol is 'a plan of the steps or stages involved in the solution of a problem' (Stratton & Hayes 1988), and the word is used to describe the text (transcription) of a think-aloud session. Ericsson & Simon's 1984 book on protocol analysis is another landmark contribution to the field.

Today's introspection differs from the nineteenth-century version in various ways. One, as Green (1998) points out, is that classical introspectionism required subjects to infer the processes whereby they came to a thought. They were asked to analyse their own cognitive processes, a major reason why subjects had to be trained in intro-spective techniques. We now recognise this as difficult if not impossible to do. Today it is normal to expect people to verbalise what they are thinking, without adding an explanatory commentary. Another dif-ference is that today many regard introspection as a useful way of generating hypotheses – providing in Woods's phrase (1996: 36) an 'initial surge of insights' – but recognise the need for other kinds of data to provide proofs for those hypotheses. The additional data may well be information not about processes, but about products (in our case the actual tasks the designers produced).

The major value of introspective verbal reports is that they enable us to examine processes that are normally hidden. They can make the covert overt. Verbal reports are nowadays used in many disciplines, particularly within the social sciences. Voss *et al.* (1983) use them to explore differences between experts and novices solving political science problems, while (as we have seen) Schoenfeld's verbal protocols record how people solve mathematical problems. Green (1998) lists some uses in the language testing area. Examiners who disagree over the assessment of an individual can be asked to think aloud while mark-ing, thereby revealing the reasons for their disagreements. A testing technique (multiple choice for example) can be scrutinised by asking subjects to introspect while using it. This enables the testers to check that the processes they predict will occur actually do so. Because the processes involved in language use are normally covert (reading and writing being the obvious examples), the technique is used a lot in language studies. Cohen & Hosenfeld (1981) provide an overview of language study work using what they call 'mentalistic data', and along with reading and writing this includes the areas of oral communication, vocabulary and test-taking ability. As well as studies of processes of language use, language learning strategy studies have also used protocol analysis widely. Introspective techniques are nowadays accepted weapons in the language researcher's armoury.

Different writers have developed their own means of classifying the various types of verbal reports. Green (1998) identifies a number of parameters along which classification may be made. One is 'temporal variation'. In *concurrent verbalisation* the subject talks while actually under-taking the process being examined, while in *retrospective verbalisation* the talking occurs afterwards. Another of Green's parameters is 'proced-ural variation'. The choice here is between *mediated* and *non-mediated*.

A verbalisation is mediated if the experimenter gives the subject some indication as to what to talk about (perhaps asking him to focus on just one aspect of the process). Hayes & Flower (1983) call this a 'directed report'. In non-mediated verbalisations the subject is free to say whatever comes into his head.

3.2.2 Verbal reports: the pros and cons

As we have seen, the major value of verbal reports is that they have the potential to make covert processes overt. Smagorinsky (1989), who provides a valuable discussion of the technique, concludes that verbal reports can 'yield significant information' about mental processes. But the technique has not been without its critics. There is a sizeable school of thought that argues that wherever possible research should be undertaken in the conditions under which the behaviour takes place 'naturally'. Irmscher (1987) is interested in the processes of writing, an area where verbal reports have been much used. 'In studying the act of writing', he says, 'investigators should ... disrupt as little as possible the natural setting of writing with cameras, tapes, and talk-aloud protocols.' The essence of the objection is that talking aloud while undertaking a mental process is an unnatural activity.

Arguments for and against 'naturalness' in data collection have occurred in many areas of research. In second language acquisition studies, for example, there were heated debates during the 1970s about whether information on the order in which learners acquire second language morphemes should be collected 'artificially' through tests, or 'naturally' by collecting data from learners as they engaged in normal conversation. One set of arguments against naturalness relates to difficulties in collecting data. Consider our own task design study as an example. We could have decided to collect data from people designing tasks as part of their work. This would have entailed finding a good number of people who did this regularly and who were prepared to be observed. We would have had to have fitted into our subjects' work schedules, waiting for the moment when they design a task. It would doubtless have taken a very long time indeed to collect sufficient natural data. Even then, the result would not necessarily be data that could be used for comparative purposes. We would have ended up with a collection of different tasks, designed over different periods of time and in different conditions. We would not, in short, have had much control over what data were collected when.

But observing task designers working naturally has great face validity. People are likely to believe that your data do indeed truly represent the processes you are studying. Herein lies the major criticism against artificial data collection, that the method used to collect data actually changes the nature of the processes being observed. This principal argument against verbal reports is suggested in research by Berkenkotter (1983). His subject was an established writer, one Donald Murray, who was asked to do some writing under different conditions. One way (the most 'natural' one) involved writing alone over a period of two months, tape recording thought processes where appropriate, and keeping notes. He was also asked to write over a period of an hour while verbalising concurrently. Murray did not take to this process: 'I have rarely felt so completely trapped and inadequate', he says (1983). 'To find equivalent feelings from my past I would have to go back to combat or to public school.' Smagorinsky (1989) accounts for this hostile reaction to verbal reports by saying that the writing task given to Murray for the concurrent verbalisation session was a particularly difficult one. But it is certainly clear that the writer did not feel concurrent verbalisation captured his natural writing behaviour.

In many 'artificial versus natural' debates, those in the artificial camp try to show that the processes revealed in experimentally collected data are essentially the same as in naturally collected data. The major objection against artificially collected data then disappears, and the advantages of artificial data collection (that it collects comparable data quickly) can win the day. The supporters of ('artificial') verbal reports have argued thus. Smagorinsky (1989: 466) surveys a number of studies that compare naturally and artificially collected data on problem solving. His conclusion: 'the cumulative results of these studies suggest that the internal structure of thought processes is not disturbed when subjects utter...verbalization' (p. 466).[2] The only proviso is that the time taken to undertake the processes may be lengthened by the subject's need to verbalise. In Ericsson & Simon's words this time: 'verbal reports...are a valuable and *thoroughly reliable* source of information about cognitive processes' (1980: 247 – italics added). Smagorinsky (1989) compares artificially and naturally collected data to writing under exam conditions and in normal situations. Exam writing is, he says, more intense, but it is comparable as a process to normal writing.

A further objection to verbal protocols is that they provide incomplete records of processes. This is partly because it is impossible for a subject to verbalise all the thoughts that enter the head, however co-operative he is being. In addition, many subjects occasionally lapse into silence. Smagorinsky (1989: 468) cites research which identifies some reasons for silences in protocols. One is that at a particular moment the cognitive load may be exceptionally high; another that subjects are attending to pieces of information especially relevant to choice of a course of action. Smagorinsky agrees that verbal reports do not give a full picture, but argues that what they do provide is far better than nothing. 'Do we need', he asks, 'to account for every mental process in order to derive helpful information about what we are studying from protocols?' (p. 469). He also makes the point that the occurrence of a silence can provide useful information, telling us that there is a moment of high cognitive load or where crucial information is being considered.

There are other problems with verbal protocols. Gilhooly (1986) finds that individuals vary considerably in how well they can do it, and this means that some individuals who may otherwise be ideal subjects, produce unrevealing protocols. It may be that Donald Murray can be dismissed as a poor concurrent verbaliser. But his case may be evidence of another problem – that some subjects, however well they may be able to verbalise concurrently, simply do not like doing it. We met both enthusiasts and critics in our study. Thus D6 announces: *I find it* [thinking aloud] *very easy, I do a lot of talking to myself.* D1's verdict on the other hand is: *I do tend to find that talking loud interferes with my thinking, I prefer to think quietly.* As we shall see below, there are others who express their unhappiness more forthrightly.

In addition there are specific problems associated with particular forms of verbal reporting. Directed reports run the risk of affecting performance (and altering natural processes) by focusing the subject's attention on particular aspects of the activity being studied. This may either help or hinder performance. Retrospective verbalisation has the disadvantage that it relies on recall, which may be both inaccurate and incomplete.

So there are arguments for and against. The researcher needs to bear both in mind. Arguments against should lead to supplementary alternative data collection methods where possible, and to a realisation of the limitations of the techniques. Perhaps the view that verbal reports are useful as hypothesis generators but not proof providers is not far from the mark. On the other hand, the researcher (and his critics) should accept that the technique can provide a great deal of information in areas where no other techniques are likely to do so. It is imperfect, but 'tis very nearly all that we have.

3.2.3   Administering concurrent verbalisation sessions

There are a number of procedures that a researcher can follow to ensure the proper conduct of concurrent verbalisation. Ericsson & Simon (1984) recommend the use of warm-up activities to give the subject some experience with what it is like to talk and think at the same time, and also to alert the researcher to any possible problems (helping to identify poor verbalisers for example). In our study we asked all our subjects to think aloud as they solved an anagram, as a way of practising concurrent verbalisation. This led to a few minor problems – some subjects expressed a dislike for anagrams and were thrown into a state of anxiety at being unable to solve ours, while others solved it so quickly as to have no real verbalisation practice. But in general the procedure sufficed: subjects spent adequate time on it, and talked aloud as they did so.

Green (1998: 11) notes that 'individuals must be discouraged from trying to explain or rationalise their thoughts'. One reason why subjects do this is that they perceive the verbalisation as 'talking to' the researcher, 'telling' the researcher what they are doing. They feel it will help the research if they attempt to explain their thoughts. Ericsson & Simon (1987: 37) use the phrase 'other-oriented description' to describe this phenomenon. It is one that we met on a number of occasions. The following example is the most explicit expression of dissatisfaction with concurrent verbalisation that we have in our data. It comes at the end of a pilot session, when the subject was asked how she felt about what she had been asked to do. Her response is an outburst:

> *I found the main problem was that I was so aware of the need to keep talking that I didn't get a chance to think anything through and I was desperate to be able to switch off, sit back, think about it in peace and quiet, think something through and I knew I was not going to be able to come up with anything, not wonderful, not even satisfactory really through this necessity to keep talking, and it is drivel. I found that if I mentioned an idea, if I hadn't had to talk about it I would have been rejecting it within seconds probably as rubbish. But because I had mentioned it I found that I was following it through, talking about it, exploring it.*

(pilot subject)

Why did she feel it necessary to talk through an idea rather than simply abandoning it? It seems likely that she felt she was thereby providing us with the data we required; she thought she was doing what she was supposed to do. What she provides is an 'other-oriented description'. She is doing this out of willingness to help, an excess of co-operation. But the result is what she sees as major disruption to her normal design processes.

We found two ways of handling this phenomenon. One was to ensure that the researcher conducting the session was not (and was not perceived as) an expert in language teaching. We made the mistake of having an applied linguist conducting some pilot sessions. The subjects knew they were in the presence of someone who knew about language teaching. The result was sometimes a kind of one-sided dialogue, where the subject drew attention to applied linguistic issues and 'discussed' them, in soliloquy (since the researcher did not join in). It must be added, though, that using non-applied linguists as interviewers was not without problems, and we have further examples of other-oriented description which may be said to have been caused by the perceived *ignorance* of the researcher interviewer. One designer, for example, feels it necessary to discourse at length on what the terms 'direct' and 'indirect speech' mean, surmising that his interviewer is unlikely to know.

The second way of handling other-oriented description is by being explicit in the initial instructions given to the subject. Krutetskii (1976) has instructions that do just this: 'Do not try to explain anything to anyone else. Pretend there is no one here but yourself. Do not tell about the solution but solve it.' We found it similarly useful to do this. Here is the interviewer explaining to D1 what he should do:

> *now while you're doing your thinking aloud on designing tasks I'm going to be taking notes but I'm not going to be looking at you and you're not talking to me OK. You're just thinking out loud.*

> (Interviewer to D1)

What do you do if your subject stops talking? In pilot protocols we were over-strict about this, asking subjects to 'keep talking' after even a short silence. A number of pilot subjects showed dissatisfaction with this, and insisted that they should have the right to periods of silence. This was particularly true of the specialists. They were (unsurprisingly) more confident than the non-specialists towards the whole procedure, and were not going to be denied periods of silent thought whatever instructions were given to them. We therefore became more tolerant of silent periods, sometimes (where it seemed appropriate) asking the subject what he *had been* thinking about during the silent period, once it was over. When a subject wanted a silent period, he would often ask for one, or simply announce that it was going to happen. On other occasions, silences would be lapsed into rather than being asked for. Then we would follow the suggestions of Ericsson & Simon (1987) and offer a reminder. The actual form of the reminder is important. Ericsson & Simon's (1987) example is that 'keep talking' is less disruptive than 'please can you tell me what you are thinking', the latter suggesting an unwanted analysis of thought processes. The example below follows directly on from what the interviewer said to D1 above. The quote also contains an example of the kind of mild objections a few designers expressed to the procedure:

> Int: ... *If you get quiet for too long I will probably say keep talking but other than that I won't get involved.*
> D1:   *I do tend to find that talking loud interferes with my thinking, I prefer to think quietly.*
> Int: *I understand that it may be a bit difficult...*
> D1:   *No I'll do my best.*

3.3   Alternative data collection methods

Our data were collected by means of concurrent verbalisation under controlled 'experimental' conditions. What other means of data collection might we have used? One of the possibilities mentioned earlier in this chapter was 'natural' design in the workplace. We discussed the logistical problems of collecting data by this method – of finding sufficient subjects who design tasks as part of their job, and who were willing to participate in the stressful process of introspection while doing that job. Had we succeeded in finding subjects we could have asked them to tape record their thought processes and keep notes – just as Murray was asked to do in the Berkenkotter study (1983) mentioned earlier. But even with the logistical difficulties overcome, there would still be the problem of data which might not offer comparisons from one individual to another, and from one group to another (S and NS/T). This is a problem which Berkenkotter, who uses Murray as a case study, did not have to face.

Another reason mentioned earlier for not collecting naturalistic data was that it may be unnecessary to do so. If, as some claim, experimentally collected concurrent verbalisation data capture the same procedures that occur in natural processing, then there is no need to confront the logistical problems of naturalistic data collection. Despite this argument, we feel that had more time and resources been available, it would indeed have been valuable to collect some data on natural design in the workplace. This would have enabled us to check whether in the task design domain the processes are indeed the same whatever the data collection method. It would also have provided a useful additional perspective on task design. The data collected would doubtless have been richer in some respects (though perhaps not in others) than the data we have. For our particular purposes we felt it preferable to used experimentally collected data, particularly because of the comparability that it provided. But a next step in the study of task design processes might usefully collect naturalistic workplace data.

A more natural way of making subjects verbalise while they design is to ask them to work in pairs. Working together necessitates talk, and the resulting verbalisation would hence be less artificial than thinking aloud into a tape and video recorder. 'Pair thinking aloud' might also relieve the stress that some subjects naturally feel when asked to put their reputation on the line by creating a task for a group of researchers. Haastrup (1987) uses the technique (in combination with other data collection methods) for the additional reason that she feels it forces subjects to provide more complete and coherent explanations than when they are working alone. Schoenfeld (1985) also considers the use of pair thinking aloud. He notes two disadvantages. One is that a partner's intervention may distort what a subject might do, forcing the latter into design procedures that are not natural for him. Secondly, when people work together, interpersonal factors (Haastrup 1987: 203 calls these 'socio-psychological variables') creep in. The resulting protocols might provide fascinating data to the psychologist of interpersonal relations, revealing a lot about how people persuade, establish power relations, take or relinquish control, negotiate meaning. They would perhaps reveal less about task design procedures. In our study we gave some subjects the option of working in pairs. None took up the offer and some individuals, particularly among the specialist group, were adamant that they were *not* prepared to work with someone else. They saw task design as a lone procedure. One informally expressed the view that producing 'tasks by committee' led to characterless materials, full of compromises. We were particularly surprised to find reluctance to work together on the part of two of our potential designers. They did not want to work as a pair, even though (or because?) they had produced a number of textbooks together! [3]

One problem with retrospective verbal reporting, mentioned earlier, is that it relies on recall, which may be both inaccurate and incomplete. Shavelson & Stern (1981) describe a technique known as 'stimulated recall'. It is particularly useful in situations where concurrent verbalisation is not possible. An example would be research into teachers' thoughts and planning processes while actually in class; clearly it is impossible for teachers to think aloud during a lesson. In stimulated recall a video tape of the lesson is played back to the teacher who taught it. He is asked to pause the tape if he has any comments to make on his own actions/thoughts during the lesson. These observations are recorded 'as a voice-over to the frozen frame of the original' (Woods 1996: 30). At the end of the process the researcher therefore has a video recorded lesson with the retrospective thoughts of the teacher. Woods uses this technique in his work on teacher cognition.

Designing a task, unlike teaching a lesson, is an activity where concurrent verbalisation is a possibility. The protocols we collected were supported by notes – those made by the designers as they worked, and those taken by the researcher during the session. These resources together in general made it possible to follow the steps in the designer's reasoning. But there were some inaudible sections, and occasions when the designer's thought processes were obscure. Stimulated recall undertaken after the concurrent verbalisation sessions would have eliminated some of these obscurities, though the extra data thus collected would have been very considerable and added to the already considerable burden of analysis. It would certainly be worth collecting some stimulated recall data in the future, to see if it adds significantly and in a cost-effective way to our understanding of task design processes.

3.4   Coding the data

3.4.1   Some points from the coding literature

Classifying and labelling natural events into discrete categories is 'a central part of most research in the social sciences' (Lampert & Ervin-Tripp 1993: 169). Its purpose is to enable the researcher to identify and group together examples of the same phenomenon, as a stage in the process of theory development. This process is called *coding*. Although forms of coding are found in quantitative studies, it is with qualitative research that the procedure is associated, particularly the work of Strauss, Glaser and others who developed the approach to qualitative analysis known as 'grounded theory' (Glaser & Strauss 1967; Strauss 1987; Strauss & Corbin 1998). Textbooks dealing with qualitative social science or educational research methods now regularly contain sections on coding, often offering useful practical advice on how to go about it. Examples textbooks are Miles & Huberman (1994), Bryman & Burgess (1994b) and Bogdan & Biklen (1992).

One of the major issues in discussions of coding relates to what is sometimes referred to in the language studies literature as the 'theory-then-research' versus 'research-then-theory' issue (see Allwright 1998). When seen in relationship to coding, this debate concerns whether, as a way of undertaking research, it is better to start off with a set of categories for analysis, which are then applied to collected data, or whether the set of categories should be allowed to emerge as the data are analysed. Some writers suggest that the researcher might bring to the data some specific codes suggested by the study's research questions; as Bogdan & Biklen (1992: 166) put it: 'particular research questions and concerns generate certain categories'. Others suggest that there may be general category types which can be made to apply to any study, whatever the domain. Frameworks proposing general category types are offered by Lofland (1971) and Bogdan & Biklen (1992); the former has code areas like *acts, activities, meanings, participation*, while the latter have *setting/context, perspectives* and *process* among others. Although these approaches have elements of 'theory-then-research', all recognise that the data themselves must play an important role in category identification. As Miles & Huberman (1994: 61) say, researchers with start lists (as these initial frameworks are called) 'know that codes will change; there is more going on out there than our initial frames have dreamed of, and few researchers are foolish enough to avoid looking for these things'.

The procedures of grounded theory are often taken as illustrative of the 'research-then-theory' position. These procedures advocate a series of steps moving from data towards theory, in what Strauss (1987: 28) calls a 'coding paradigm'. The first stage of the paradigm is so-called *open coding*. This is a 'process of breaking down, examining, comparing, conceptualising, and categorizing data' (Strauss & Corbin 1990: 61). It is a kind of brainstorming activity, based on careful analysis of the data, and allowing the researcher some freedom to code as appears appropriate at the time, in the knowledge that changes to the coding system are sure to occur later. Once the data have been 'broken down' by the open coding process, the next stage uses *axial codes* which involve 'intense analysis done around one category [or 'axis'] at a time' (Strauss 1987: 32). In this way detailed analysis is invested in various categories that have emerged during the analysis. Then follows *selective coding* in which important, core codes are identified and expanded. By the end of these stages the beginnings of a theory should be emerging, from what started off as a relatively free coding procedure. One way of viewing the paradigm, following Bryman & Burgess (1994a), is to conceptualise it as fragmentation (the 'breaking down' in open coding) followed by 'the gradual *building up* of categories out of the data' (Bryman & Burgess 1994: 5, italics added) – a process of analysis followed by synthesis.

Though grounded theory's procedures seem in line with the 'research-then-theory' position, Bryman & Burgess (1994a) remind us that the original version of the theory (in Glaser & Strauss 1967 for example) was in fact proposing a cyclical procedure of moving continually during analysis from data towards theory and back again. As an example of this cyclical movement, Bryman & Burgess (1994a: 5) cite the work of Sutton on dying. We shall quote Sutton at some length, because it is relevant to the approach we took. His analysis, he says,

> ... entailed continuous comparison of data and model throughout the research project. I began the research by developing a rough working framework based on the existing literature, conversations with colleagues, and pilot interviews. I travelled back and forth between the emerging model and evidence throughout the data gathering and writing. In doing so, some elements suggested by the literature and prior intuitions could be grounded in evidence, while others could not. Other elements proposed at the outset or suggested by a subset of cases were retained but were modified considerably to conform to the evidence.
>
> (Sutton 1987: 547)

Rather than being 'research-then-theory', the procedure is closer to 'theory-then-research-then-theory (-then-research)...'. It is the same kind of procedure that Miles & Huberman (1994: 65) have in mind when they speak of 'iterative cycles of induction and deduction', and that I call, in Johnson (2001b), 'complementary cyclical development'.

3.4.2   Coding task design data

Coding is a difficult task at the best of times. It is also time-consuming, according to Miles & Huberman (1994: 56) taking from twice to five times as long as actual data collection. With data as heterogeneous as ours, it is a very challenging and lengthy business indeed. In this section we shall look briefly and selectively at some of the coding issues which became salient in the analysis of our particular data set. We discuss four issues. The section finishes with a consideration of the strategy used to arrive at our list of codes.

Code selection

Bogdan & Biklen (1992: 165) begin their discussion of coding in the following way. 'Imagine', they suggest, 'a large gymnasium in which thousands of toys are spread out on the floor. You are given the task of sorting them into piles according to a scheme that you are to develop. You walk around the gym looking at the toys, picking them up, and examining them.' You note that there are very many different ways of putting the toys into piles, some of those suggested by Bogdan & Biklen being according to size, colour, country of origin, date manufactured, the type of play they encourage, and the age group they suit.

'Such an activity approaches', Bogdan & Biklen say, 'what a qualitative researcher does to develop a coding system to organize data, although the task is more difficult.' Thus (in the domain which concerns us), one may take part of a task design protocol and accurately associate with it any number of codes. Note the word 'accurately'. Just as all the various toy categorisations mentioned above would, if done properly, be accurate (in the sense of not presenting false information), so too may any number of protocol codes present information contained in the text. An example will illustrate. Just before the extract below, D1 has proposed a task in which learners describe to each other ideal or least ideal people in various categories (e.g. 'what would your ideal/least ideal doctor be like?'). D1 now comes up with an alternative possibility:

> *So another possible task that occurs to me at this stage is the idea of getting students to invent a character for a soap opera. This is a rather different type of task, in that in the original one I was thinking of, of describing your ideal or least ideal person in different guises it's likely to be a rather more spontaneous activity and will involve the people talking to other members of the class more or less at the same time so you could get people to just think about their ideas for a while and then talk to somebody else in the class about it. Describe, so you could have that done in pairs so you would have a lot more speaking going on. With this one of inventing a character for a soap opera that's likely to be a sort of task where you get people in groups to discuss and come up with a character and then present that character to the class. So it's a rather different nature of task I'm not sure we would have time for it.*

(D1)

Miles & Huberman (1994: 56) note that 'what you "see" in a transcription is inescapably selective. A critical theorist sees different things than a deconstructivist or a symbolic interactionist does', and it would be easy to imagine quite different codings of this extract according to perspective. Consider for example how a syntactician might analyse it, in comparison with a discourse analyst. But even supposing a common set of aims – to look, as we are, at task design procedures – it still remains the case that many different codings are possible.

The basic outline of this passage is fairly clear: D1 proposes an alternative task type, involving description of characters in a soap opera. He compares this alternative with his previous idea of describing ideal/least ideal people, and at the end of the extract notes a problem with his new proposal – the amount of class time the task would occupy. Soon after the passage above he in fact decides against the alternative, saying *so we'll scrub that idea because it doesn't fit in with the time constraints available*. But although the outline is clear, innumerable problems emerge when we come to consider actual codes. In the first few lines he is proposing an alternative task type. The verb *propose* is quite appropriate as a code here. But so too are *consider* and *identify*, and even *describe* perhaps. Instead of *alternative* one might equally well have *modification*. There are also issues regarding whether what he is describing is best called a *task type* – in the course of the study many different ways of describing tasks emerged: *type* is one of them, *scenario* another. Or is what he is proposing really just a difference in the person being described (the change from ideal/least ideal person to soap opera character)? This might suggest a coding along the lines of *propose describee modification*. He then *compares alternatives*. What he is also doing is *developing* (or *expanding*, or even *considering*) the *scenario/task type*. Which of these phrases should be used in the coding? D1 then ponders *event sequences* (thinking and speaking), and mentions criteria such as *spontaneity* and *quantity of speech*. Finally he identifies a *problem* (or *issue*, or *disadvantage*?) with the *task type/scenario/describee type* – that it will take up a lot of time. The problem relates to the *constraints* on the task given in the design brief. The whole of the latter half of the passage may be seen as involving an *evaluation* of the *alternative scenario*. All the alternative wordings that fill this paragraph are accurate; they all describe what occurs in the text. But clearly not all these alternatives can make their way into the coding of the passage. Choices have to be made. Coding is a highly selective process.

How may coding choices be made? Sometimes it is a (comparatively) simple issue of selecting codes that will have more utility in terms of the data set as a whole. As an example of the processes involved here, we initially introduced the term *problem* as a code. We then discovered that alongside 'problems' there were also 'issues'. These are topics raised for discussion, not necessarily initially as problems, but which might lead to some modification being made to a task. For a while both *problem* and *issue* were used as codes. Then it was decided that the one term *issue* would suffice for both, and *problem* was dropped. Similarly, as analysis of the protocol set proceeded it was found useful to distinguish *task type* from *task scenario* (just how is described in the list of codes in Appendix 1). According to the way we draw this distinction what is described in the extract above is an alternative *scenario*.

But often it is more than a question of terminology, and other choices involve more substantial decisions. Do we characterise these events as describing a *scenario* or an *alternative*? Is it, in other words, important to signal that an alternative is being considered here? And is it important for us to note that the problem identified with the alternative relates to a *task constraint* given in the design brief? The answers can only be given in terms of the research questions we are asking, and the potential significance of the factors involved. In the case of both these examples one can very well imagine that the choice of coding will either mask or reveal significant findings. It just might be, for example, that S designers consider many more alternatives than NS/T designers; identification of alternatives may be significant specialist task design behaviour, and this will only be revealed if alternatives are signalled in the coding. Equally, it may be that when evaluating a possible task/scenario, some designers are more sensitive to 'task constraints' mentioned in the brief (for example the constraint that the task must be no more than 30 minutes long), while other designers are more sensitive to 'learner-related constraints' (e.g. that learners in a particular cultural context are not encouraged to talk too much in class). Once again, we can only make such findings if we code the kinds of constraints (task or learner-related) that designers attend to.

How do we know in advance what it is worth looking for? As Miles & Huberman (1994: 55) put it: 'if you don't know what matters more, everything matters'. But you cannot code for everything that might matter! In some applied language study areas important issues will already have been raised in the literature, and this will suggest areas worth focusing on. There is little literature on task design to help in this way, though studies like Schoenfeld's (1985) do raise relevant issues. For example, he discusses metacognition (or 'control' as he calls it) at length in relation to mathematics problem solving. His discussion, plus similar treatments in other domains, suggest that it is worth coding metacognitive or control behaviour. But such help aside, one has to rely (in the manner of grounded theory) on one's emerging instincts as to what the issues involved are likely to be. Attending to emerging instincts is of course a highly time-consuming process. It is also a highly frustrating one, particularly when instincts emerge late in the day and suggest the introduction of new codes into masses of data already analysed. In exploratory studies such as this one, it is a sad truth that one is in the best position to know what one is looking for when the analysis has been finished and the coding done. At various points in this study we have had the feeling that an insightful set of codes might be an appropriate finishing – not starting – point. These issues to do with how to select codes are covered in more detail in Johnson (2001b).

Making coding insightful

In his description of how coding should be done in grounded theory, Strauss (1987) argues eloquently for examination of the data which is both *close* and *interpretative*. The procedure he illustrates begins with a careful, highly detailed, even word by word, examination of the data. This must be *close* to ensure that whatever theories eventually emerge will be truly grounded in the data. But as one proceeds from open through axial to selective coding, the analysis must become increasingly *interpretative*. 'The common tendency', Strauss notes (1987: 29), 'is simply to take a bit of the data...and translate that into a précis of it.' Having been immersed in the materials at the open coding stage, the researcher has to stand back from them, abstract out of them if insightful coding is to occur. It is unfortunately extremely easy to code uninsightfully.

In our experience uninsightful coding is often the result of looking at events individually and out of context – simply coding what occurs on a line-by-line basis. The result may be an account of the protocol which, although not inaccurate, reveals nothing insightful about what is really going on. To take an example from the extract given earlier: a comparison (of chosen scenario and proposed alternative) occurs in the extract, and a *compare* code may represent this. But the crucial fact is that the comparison is undertaken for the purposes of evaluation. D1 is comparing scenarios in order to evaluate whether the alternative is worth adopting. Indeed it becomes clear in D1's protocol as a whole that a major design strategy he follows is to propose alternative ways of doing these things, then to evaluate these alternatives by comparing them with an already discussed idea, leading to an acceptance or rejection of the alternative. In this particular instance it may or may not be that there is a place for a *compare* code. The point is that the main code, which must appear somewhere, is *evaluate*. Noting the comparison without its evaluative intention would be uninsightful. As a further example, consider the procedure of 'identifying issues or problems', something that designers do all the time. But they have various reasons for doing this. On occasions issues may be identified as part of an evaluative process, in a sequence of moves in which the designer is trying to arrive at a suitable task and is dismissing unsuitable ones, as problems become apparent with them. On other occasions, issues are identified at a point when a task has been selected for final development. As part of that development, the designer may identify issues for which solutions are then sought, as part of a developmental rather than an evaluative process. Again, coding *identify issue* without noting why it occurs would be unrevealing.

Our experience is that on many occasions the answer to how to avoid uninsightful coding is to code in an aggressively top-down way, such that smaller units are always seen in relation to the larger ones that point their meaning. To achieve this, following a period of initial open coding, each design protocol was first divided into major stages, identifying the large movements in the design process. Only when this was done were lower levels analysed. A coding rule emerged which came to be followed slavishly: no unit was coded until the larger unit in which it occurred was assigned a code.

Multiple coding

Mention was made earlier of how a number of codes can apply to the same stretch of language, and that a selective process is needed when deciding on codes. But the result of that selective process need not be assignment of just one code to a unit. Indeed, a restriction like this would reflect a lack of understanding about how language is used. As is well discussed in the linguistics literature, it is the nature of discourse to be multifunctional, such that any one utterance may carry more than one 'meaning'. Of course, care is needed to ensure that multiple codings are not the result of a coding system which is slipshod and contains unnecessary overlaps. But with this guarded against, it is entirely legitimate to code an utterance in more than one way. We therefore agree with Lampert & Ervin-Tripp (1993: 180) when they say that 'given the plurifunctionality pervading language, double coding may not only be useful, but desirable'. In the days of pencil-and-paper analysis, multiple codings could present logistical problems, but in computer coding these problems do not exist.

Adding a quantitative dimension

In early analyses of parts of the data (as in Johnson 2000 for example), we added a small amount of quantitative analysis to our essentially qualitative approach – almost inevitable given our interest in comparing two groups (S and NS/T designers). On a number of occasions we found that the results suggested by quantitative analysis were at odds with our emerging feelings as to what was in fact occurring in the data. An example will clarify one major reason for this. At a particular point we were interested in the decision-making procedures of the two groups, this interest being based on the informal observation that S designers seemed to create more points at which decisions had to be made, and would then proceed to make them. In order to investigate this, we counted all instances of two particularly relevant codes: <u>fix</u> (where decisions to adopt something are made) and <u>reject</u> (where something is discounted – all codes are explained in Appendix 1). The resulting numbers did not seem to match this informal observation. We then realised that some other codes implied decision-making but were not included in the analysis because the decision-making element was not sufficiently explicit. This was particularly the case for a code which we subsequently dropped: <u>establish</u>. This code really means 'consider and then decide on', and indeed we later replaced it with <u>consider</u> plus <u>fix</u>. The lesson we take from this concurs with that of Miles & Huberman (1994: 56), that: 'converting words into numbers and then tossing away the words gets a researcher into all kinds of mischief'.

3.4.3   Arriving at a code list

In our brief survey of the coding literature, mention has been made of various ways of developing codes. The method we followed was close to that associated with grounded theory and involved what Johnson (2001b) calls 'complementary cyclical development' (Miles & Huberman's 'iterative cycles of induction and deduction'). The procedure involved approaching each protocol as an individual case, at first deliberately avoiding any search for generalisable categories. So Protocol 1 and then Protocol 2 were assigned open codes without any attempt to find common categories. But then with two protocols coded, thought was given to possible similarities, and this invariably led to modifications in the initial coding. Protocols were then added one by one, first being viewed as individual cases, then with generalisations being sought which led to modifications in all coding already done. With 16 protocols the process was ferociously time-consuming. In effect it entailed 16 recoding operations, each time changing codes already assigned to more and more data. But the end result is coding that is grounded in the data but at the same time achieves generalisations. It is important that the dialectic is here two-way. The movement is from particular pieces of data to generalisable codes in the first place. But then as more protocols are considered, emerging theory begins to colour how particular protocols are regarded.

3.5   Development of 'TADECS'

3.5.1   The building blocks

The system developed to describe task design behaviour is called TADECS, for Task Design Coding System. Though based loosely on a number of existing systems, including Ball *et al.* (1997), it has largely been developed with the specific concerns of task design in mind. The system uses two category types, known as *operators* and *referents*. Operators are 'cognitive activities', and appear as verbs describing actions. Examples are <u>monitor</u>, <u>compare</u>, <u>abandon</u>, <u>read</u> and <u>write</u>. Operators comprise a relatively small set, of less than 30 items. The list of referents is very much longer. These are characteristically noun phrases describing topics which interest us. To exemplify referents: one is called <u>cultural sensitivity</u>, under which fall all comments where designers discuss characteristics of particular cultural groups. Several designers note, for example, that in many cultures there are great sensitivities associated with the description of a person's physical attributes. A second example referent is <u>authenticity</u>, under which are coded all references by designers to the issue of ensuring that a task is 'authentic' in any of a number of ways, including in terms of its language content, or the activities it involves. Referents are grouped into 'families'. One large family, for example, is called 'design brief-related'. This family includes a number of codes concerned with discussion of the design brief. Two example codes are <u>age</u> (the learners are specified as adults) and <u>level</u> (the learners are intermediate). Many of the codes in this family related to points mentioned in the brief itself. Some, however, deal with points not actually mentioned, but raised in discussion of the brief.[4]

In the descriptions of specific stretches of discourse, operators usually combine with referents, in verb + noun phrase sequences. Examples are: <u>review brief</u>, where the designer goes back over the design brief to check some aspect of what is required, and <u>evaluate task</u>, where the designer undertakes an evaluation of the task he has designed. TADECS is found in full in Appendix 1, where the individual codes are given working definitions.

As argued earlier, particular importance was placed on the identification and coding of large units of discourse. Schoenfeld (1985: 286) makes the point in relation to mathematics problem solving that although researchers have developed sometimes lengthy 'process code dictionaries', these generally deal with detailed analysis of protocols, while little has been done to develop 'macroanalyses', which reveal the major episodes in a protocol. He develops his own macroanalysis model, and TADECS has much in common with this. Our highest level of analysis, called the *macrostage*, identifies the main episodes in the design process. We recognise just six macrostages.[5] These appear in Appendix 1 but are given in Figure 3.2 for convenience. As might be

Read brief:	Where the designer, following what the interviewer requests, reads the design brief aloud
Analyse:	Where important elements of what is to be done are identified. The stage characteristically ends with the identification of some entity (e.g. a task type or an actual scenario) which then leads into the next stage, where it is developed, along with other alternatives
Explore:	Where different types of solution may be considered and one task type/scenario is decided on as a final choice for detailed development
Instantiate:	Where the designer adds flesh to the chosen skeleton
Write WS	The designer composes the Worksheet(s) to go with his/her task
Write TN	Composing the accompanying Teachers' Notes

Figure 3.2   The TADECS macrostages

expected, not all designers follow this sequence in anything like a rigorous way. Some, for example, read the brief and recall a task they have used before, which they immediately instantiate. Sometimes it is impossible to say where *Analyse* ends and *Explore* begins. Nevertheless, the sequence is generally applicable to most protocols, and it does provide a workable framework for analysis.

At the other end of the size scale are small elements roughly akin to the 'acts' in Sinclair & Coulthard (1975), and which we call *events*. These elements usually (but not always, because as discussed earlier we do allow multiple coding) deal with one issue. For example, at some point in the design process there may be a series of events dealing with timing. These might be <u>propose timing</u> (where a particular time span is allocated for part of an activity), followed later by <u>modify timing</u> (where the proposed timing is modified in the light of some discussed factor), and finally by <u>fix timing</u> (where a final decision about timing is made).

For many stretches of discourse it was also found useful to identify an intermediate level of analysis between *macrostage* and *event*. We call them *microstages*, and they are roughly equivalent to the 'move' in the Sinclair & Coulthard model. As an example of this middle level, the events mentioned above concerned with timing would go together to form a larger unit which might be coded as <u>consider timing</u>. For convenience of identification, macrostages are written in italics, while microstages and events are underlined.

In one of our modes of analysis, to be described below, we find it necessary to identify further descriptive elements. We call these *specifications*. Here is an example taken from the analysis of D12's protocol.

At the point in question he is instantiating his task, and is going over one particular stage, checking the details of what he has proposed. We code this event as <u>review stage</u>. But we wish to add details specifying what aspects of the stage he is particularly concerned with, so we add the codes <u>teacher action</u>, <u>learner action</u> and <u>timing</u>. This indicates that the designer is reviewing a stage of his task in terms of what the teacher and learners do, and in terms of the time it takes. A shorthand way of representing this would be <u>review stage</u>: <u>teacher action</u>; <u>learner action</u>; <u>timing</u>, where the specifications follow the colon. In this case, the relation which holds between event code and specifications is one of 'in terms of', but in other cases different relationships hold. The code-specification sequence <u>evaluate task: negative</u>, for example, indicates that the designer is evaluating his task in a negative way. We agonised about the variety of relationships holding between codes and specifications, initially feeling that a rigorous analytical model would introduce different categories for these different relationships. But our conclusion was that introducing a large number of semantically rigorous categories would have resulted in unwieldy analysis, providing all kinds of accurate but unuseful information.

3.5.2 The model itself

We wanted TADECS to provide two general sorts of information about task design. Firstly we were interested in the procedures followed, and needed a model that would provide easy retrieval of procedural information concerning design stages, and the order in which events occurred. But we also required information about a host of topics of potential interest. An example might be given regarding the <u>cultural sensitivity</u> referent mentioned earlier. We had an initial suspicion that maybe NS/T designers, as teachers, were more sensitive to cultural differences than S designers, many of whom produced materials for a global market and could not afford to attend to cultural differences among learners world wide. To explore the validity of this view, we needed to be able to collect together instances of this and similar codes.

We hoped that the codes identified in TADECS would potentially allow both these general aims to be met. But we found that different ways of representing our analysis would best meet these two aims. As regards the second aim, we used ATLAS.ti as a means of carrying out the analysis of all protocols. This software, well accepted in social science (including language study) research, enables codes of differing sizes to be attached to stretches of discourse. Collecting instances of the same codes, or code families, over a group of protocols (in our case the two

[*Event number*]	[*Macrostage*]	[*Microstage*]
Operator		
Referent		
Specification		
Subsidiary		
Result		
Notes		

Figure 3.3   The action box template

main groups are of course S and NS/T designers) becomes an easy task, and various other operations allowed by the software facilitate other aspects of analysis. For those unfamiliar with ATLAS.ti, a short example of analysis of part of one protocol is given in Appendix 2.

Although almost all the information needed for the analysis of major movements in the design process is contained in the ATLAS.ti representations, these were in fact produced as a final stage of this part of the analysis. Preceding that, we found it useful to represent what was occurring in terms of what we called *action boxes* which made it easier to discern large movements in the protocols. Action boxes have the form shown in Figure 3.3.

In row 1 the first column numbers the event according to where it occurs in the protocol. Columns 2 and 3 indicate the macro- and microstages within which the event occurs. Rows 2, 3 and 4 are self-explanatory. 'Subsidiary' (row 5) allows for multiple coding of the event, and contains any other coding that is occurring along with the main coding. The 'Result' row (row 6) usually contains a number referring to another event (often the immediately following one) which occurs as a result of the present event. This enables decision-making processes and dependencies between events to be plotted. The final row ('Notes') allows for any observations on the part of the coder. Appendix 3 shows a series of action boxes describing a number of events. Figure 3.4 illustrates for just one event (in D15's protocol). It tells us that this is the 40th event in D15's protocol. He is at the macrostage of instantiating his final task, which he has decided on, and in this microstage is now developing the main part of his task, the 'main activity' (he has just finished designing a preparatory phase). At this point he realises there is a problem regarding who the learners are being asked to describe. It is a classmate, and the problem is that learners may feel

40	*Instantiate*	*Develop stage: main activity*
Operator	Identify	
Referent	Issue	
Specification	Describee: classmate; touchiness	
Subsidiary	Identify condition: togetherness	
Result	41	
Notes	Recognises the danger of touchiness, but says it depends on how well the class gets on. This leads him to the modification in 41	

Figure 3.4   An example action box

embarrassed about describing someone in the class (or may indeed offend the classmate by an uncomplimentary description). At the same time D15 recognises that this is only an issue if the class members do not know each other very well, or do not get on. These considerations lead the designer to modify describee in event 41, changing the describee from classmate to famous person.

Action boxes provide an accessible account of the main design movements. Each event has an associated action box, and this means that there are usually between 70 and 110 per protocol. Given this high number, it was found useful also to produce *action box summaries*. These contain one box per microstage and show within each box the associated string of events. These summaries thus show the main design procedures in just one or two pages, and provide a broad summary view of procedures the designer has followed. Chapter 4 contains examples of action box summaries.

4
A Look at Two Designers

In Chapters 5 and 6 we shall look in detail at the design behaviour of our subjects. But before descending into detail it will be useful to provide a sense of how designers work through the design process from beginning to end. In this chapter we shall therefore concentrate on two designers – one from the S category and one NS/T. The particular designers, D1 and D12, have been selected as representatives to exemplify some typical design behaviours of the two groups, and although one aim is certainly to show contrasts between these, D1 and D12 have not been chosen because they are the best and worst of the two categories. D12 is very far from being a straw man, set up to contrast unfavourably with the good practices of D1. Since these two designers are referred to constantly throughout this chapter, they have been given pseudonyms to replace their numbers. D1 will be known as George, and D12 as Colin. These pseudonyms will be used in this chapter only. The final versions of all the designers' tasks are to be found in Appendix 6.

Some other conventions: direct quotations from the protocols are put in italics, and (unless very long) appear as 'running quotations'. In order to help familiarise readers with the coding system, key code words are sometimes (where felt appropriate) underlined on first occurrence. These words appear as various parts of speech, and words which as codes belong together may be separated in the text. So what is coded as identify procedure may appear as 'identifies the procedure'. In the interests of readability, the protocols are described in normal text (as if part of a narrative). Occasional action box summaries are included for George but not Colin, partly to clarify the overall shape of the design process, and partly to illustrate what these summaries look like. Since the main aim of this chapter is to provide an overall view, detailed discussion will be avoided, though some characteristics are inevitably drawn attention to, often in preparation for further discussion in Chapters 5 and 6. Sometimes these are given labels which appear in inverted commas. For example, the term 'concrete visualisation capacity' is given to the characteristic of being able rapidly to envisage possible candidate tasks in some detail.

4.1   An S designer's protocol (D1 – George)

The interview with George is conducted by one of the ESRC research group team. It takes place in the Psychology Department of the University of Lancaster. The interview room is equipped with audio and video taping facilities, and there is an adjacent studio in which another of the researchers sits, controlling the recording equipment. Between the two rooms is a one-way mirror, such that the researcher in the studio can see interviewer and interviewee, but not vice versa.

The interviewer begins by asking George about his task design experience. He describes how he began by having to teach a group of ESP students for whom there were no suitable ready-made materials; so he designed his own. He then went abroad and worked with an overseas team producing materials for local use. This experience led to him being commissioned to write a textbook by a UK publisher. Since then he has become well known as a textbook writer (though modesty prevents him from mentioning this).

Following this short introduction, the interviewer explains that she is going to give George an anagram to solve, to provide practice at concurrent verbalisation. He agrees readily, and in fact solves the anagram in a very short time. The interviewer then explains how the think-aloud session will be conducted (her exact words are cited on p. 39): she will take notes but not look at him; he needs to remember that he is talking to himself, not to her; if there is a silence, she will prompt him to continue talking. George agrees to do his best, though he expresses some worries about the think-aloud procedure (what he says has again been cited before, on p. 37). The interviewer tries to put his mind at rest by saying:

> *Int*:   ... *where you really feel that* [concurrent verbalisation] *is interfering with your thinking feel free to say so and take a few seconds if you need to think quietly. If I feel I need some insight as to what you're thinking about then I'll say keep talking at that point OK? So if you'll just read that* [the design brief] *aloud* ...

George co-operates by reading the design brief (given on p. 29) aloud. Having done this, he (like many other designers) asks if he can read the brief through again silently to himself, observing that he finds it difficult to take in information while reading aloud (coded as identify modus operandi). He then immediately identifies the procedure he will follow in his design, to think of a purpose for the activity: *are we, for example, getting them to describe pictures that they can see, to describe somebody that they know? So that would be one thing I'd have to sort out.* The other thing he says he must 'sort out' is what genre to use. Will it be an information gap activity, for example? He then identifies three issues, which he presents as problems. One is that *when you think about real life there aren't that many times when you actually go about producing some sort of long description of people.* Secondly, he notes (rightly or wrongly) that for some nationalities physical description is a problem because of similarities in looks between people. The third issue he identifies is that where both physical and character description is concerned there is the danger of causing offence if the describee is a person present (such as a class member, who might cruelly be described as having big ears, for example, or not being particularly intelligent). This leads him to a solution (solve issue), namely to involve describees who are not present. Note that at least two of the three constraints he mentions are to do with the learners and their context, and indicate a characteristic which might be called 'learner/context sensitivity'. He concludes consideration of these concerns with a metalinguistic summary: *so these are some of the constraints that I might be working under trying to find a task which would achieve the ends but also meet these constraints, those problems.* He then has a quiet think, as a result of which he identifies another issue which will need attention. It is based on the information transfer genre which he clearly has in mind, where learners describe people to each other and have to guess who the describee is. The problem is that unless care is taken, it will be possible to identify the describee very quickly. For example, if a person is described as wearing glasses, that may narrow down the field to just one or two; so the activity may not take very long. Unlike the earlier constraints he has been considering, he is here concerned not with 'learner/context sensitivity' but with 'task logistics sensitivity'. In other words, it is his familiarity with the information transfer genre that leads him to identify a possible problem at this stage. His conclusion is that he needs to find an activity where lots of language is needed for identification of the describee to take place. We here witness a characteristic of S designers, that their consideration of problematic issues often leads directly to stated implications for task

1. **Read brief**

2. **Analyse**
(a) Identify modus operandi: silent reading
(b) Identify procedure: purpose; genre
(c) Identify issue: activity unreality; physical similarities
(d) Identify issue: describee: classmate; solve issue: [*a non-present person*][1]
(e) Identify state of play: done
(f) Quiet think; identify issue: easy resolution; solve issue: participation level
(g) Quiet think; fix describee: imaginary person

Figure 4.1   Action box summary of George's *Read brief* and *Analyse* stages

design. We call this characteristic 'consequence identification'. There then follows a further period of silent thought, and at the end of this he announces a decision that marks the end of the *Analyse* macrostage: *right so what I think I would have is a context where we are describing an imaginary person.* His *Explore* stage now begins.

Figure 4.1 is an action box summary of the *Read brief* and *Analyse* stages we have just been discussing.

Having decided on this task <u>type</u>, George immediately finds a problem with it, that the <u>language content</u>, possibly involving structures like 'would be', might be too difficult for the learners. But he <u>checks</u> back to the <u>brief</u>, confirms that the learners are at intermediate level, and dismisses this problem. He then starts to think in more detail about the describee. His first thought is that the learners might be asked to describe ideal people – an ideal doctor, bank manager, spouse and so on. It soon occurs to him to include 'least ideal' as well – *the kind of doctor you wouldn't like to have to go to see*, the bank manager you'd hate to have to ask for a loan from. He <u>evaluates</u> this alternative, decides it would add an element of fun to the task, and then apparently <u>fixes</u> the <u>describee</u>. But he has not finished with his consideration of possible task types or scenarios, and he now considers another possibility. Perhaps learners could be asked to imagine that techniques of genetic engineering have made it possible to produce the perfect baby. What characteristics would their perfect baby have? But he soon dismisses this possibility as being *a bit too complicated*, and returns to the describing ideal/least ideal scenario.

George now sets about identifying categories of possible describees. He goes through a long list of possibilities, including boyfriend/ girlfriend, doctor, bank manager, teacher, parent, best friend, and even airline pilot. Throughout this process he constantly evaluates the potential categories. Sometimes possible describees are eliminated for a reason to do with task logistics. He decides for example that the characteristics of the ideal bank manager and doctor might be very similar, hence that only one of the two should be included. Sometimes issues raised are sociocultural. For example, he is aware that in some contexts discussion of the ideal teacher might cause embarrassment, with learners being led to unflattering contrasts between ideal and actually existing! After his lengthy consideration of possible describees he <u>identifies</u> the <u>state of play</u> reached: *OK so we'd have something like that where we've got to describe this kind of person and we want to describe them in terms of their physical appearance, and also character or personality. Right.* A lengthy extract from this portion of George's protocol is illustrated in Chapter 6 (p. 105).

What happens next is something that often occurs in the data after a metacognitive statement of <u>state of play</u> – a change of direction or a movement forward. In this case it leads George to consider the possibility of a quite new possible scenario. The words immediately following those above are: *while I am doing this actually, another possibility does strike me . . . and that would be inventing a character for a soap opera or something like that.* It is characteristic of S designers that even though they may be well along the road of developing one possible scenario (so that in fact we seem to be at the *Instantiate* stage), they are still in fact in *Explore*, and open to a consideration of new scenarios. George now compares the two possible scenarios, 'inventing a soap opera character' versus 'describing ideal/least ideal people'. His evaluation of the scenarios is detailed and very concrete, being concerned *inter alia* with the different classroom <u>configurations</u> that might be involved in each, how these would affect the amount of language used and whether within them the learners would be tempted to use their mother tongue (this problem area is coded as <u>L1 use</u>). But his main problem with the soap opera idea is that it would be very time-consuming. He works through this objection in detail, and ends up rejecting the possible scenario: *well if you've got 15 to 20 learners you're going to have what, 5 groups, each of them need a couple of, 3 or 4 minutes to present so that's nearly 20 minutes gone just in the presentation stage which gives you very little time to actually plan so we'll scrub that idea because it doesn't fit in with the time constraints available. So we will go back to the ideal and least ideal thing.*

Back with the ideal/least ideal scenario, George now begins to sketch out a <u>framework</u> for the activity. Out of the comparative evaluation of the two scenarios he has just finished comes the decision that pairwork will be involved. This might be regarded as an instance of opportunistic decision-making – a configuration decision emerging from a comparative evaluation. What he then does is characteristic of the behaviour of S designers, and is coded as <u>simulate output</u>. George imagines, and verbalises, exactly what he thinks the learners will say when undertaking part of the task. Here is just part of this process: *so they* [the learners] *would say – 'well my ideal girlfriend would be quite tall', 'she would have fair hair', I don't mind what colour eyes she's got', that sort of thing.* As a result of this simulation, his earlier concerns about language level return. But as before, he decides that the intermediate level learners should be able to handle the linguistic demands. So now, after all the twists and turns occurring during the *Explore* stage, he decides that this will be his final task. *Explore* ends with a perfect example of a metalinguistic <u>state of play</u> statement leading straight into *Instantiate*. He is summarising what has been decided and what needs to be done next:

> *we'll go with that. So we're having ideal/least ideal – these categories. They're going to think about some ideas first of all and then they're going to get together with somebody else in the class and just exchange information about what they are and discuss any new differences. Right so now we need to actually put down some ideas on this.*

Figure 4.2 shows an action box summary of George's *Explore* stage. George approaches the instantiation of his task by writing a worksheet (<u>WS</u>) containing instructions or rubrics for the learners. He identifies the <u>stages</u> of his task – a <u>preparation</u> stage at which learners think about what they will say, and a <u>main activity</u> in which they give and

---

3	**Explore**
(a)	Identify issue: language content; check brief: level; maintain scenario
(b)	Consider describee: [*ideal person*]
(c)	Consider describee: [*least ideal person*]; evaluate describee: interest level; fix describee
(d)	Identify scenario: [*genetic engineering*]; describe; evaluate; reject
(e)	Consider describee; evaluate; fix; identify state of play: done
(f)	Identify scenario: [*soap opera*]; compare scenario: configuration; L1 use; evaluate scenario: [*soap opera*]: timing; reject scenario
(g)	Develop framework; fix configuration: pairwork
(h)	Simulate output; identify issue: level; maintain scenario
(i)	Fix scenario: describee; framework; identify state of play: done, to be done

Figure 4.2   Action box summary of George's *Explore* stage

receive information with partners in pairs. As George begins to write his WS instructions, he discourses at some length on the problems of rubric writing, in particular the issue of whether to address learners directly ('you'), or indirectly ('he/she'). We code such discourse as philosophise. As with nearly all designers, writing instructions for the WS or TN (the code for teachers' notes) reveals many detailed logistical problems with tasks and often leads to their revision. Indeed, many designers use the process of WS or TN writing as a major way of instantiating tasks.

In the case of George, the first issue he confronts is how many ideal/ least ideal people learners should describe, given that the description of one person will not take very long. He works through a number of possibilities. Here, as throughout his protocol, he shows great ability to envisage each possibility in great detail. This characteristic, which we call 'concrete visualisation capacity', may be an important characteristic of expert design and is worth illustrating in detail. In the following extract it is not necessary fully to appreciate the nature of the proposal he is making, or of the alternatives which he goes on to consider. What is important is the kind of concrete detail the designer is able to visualise. The extract also, incidentally, illustrates George's ability to choose between alternative choices by reference to what is required by the brief, thus indicating that his decision-making is principled:

> *...we could do that in two ways. We could either have Student A where you choose one of the categories, boyfriend, girlfriend for example, Student A tells and then Student B tells and then we can either have the next category, or at that point we might say – 'Move on find another partner and choose another category of person' and that might actually fit the brief rather better because you want to let them interact as much as possible with as many different members of the class involved, so* [reading from brief] *oh 'as many different members of the class involved' so it doesn't really matter if they are interacting with the same person as much as possible and they are all doing it at the same time, that's all right, well we're still within the brief.*

The next 16 minutes are taken up with completing the WS. George does this methodically, describing each stage of his task in turn. We shall not here describe this process blow by blow, but will instead draw attention to the following six characteristics:

(a)   he returns often to the problems of rubric writing, and philosophises freely on it.[2] One of his main concerns is how to make the language simple. For example, he needs to refer to 'categories of describees', and spends time considering how to avoid the difficult word 'category';

(b) another issue related to rubric writing concerns what should go on the WS and what in the TN. His personal view: *I find it easier to have the bones of the task with the students as well and then the teachers' notes are an expansion of that*;

(c) he continues to show sensitivity to the constraints of task design (we earlier called this 'task logistics sensitivity'). An issue that concerns him, for example, is to set the task up such that the describees are sufficiently dissimilar to ensure there is no overlap in language output;

(d) he regularly summarises the state of play reached, and equally regularly reads over the WS text so far written. These summaries lead either to modifications in the text (which may involve changes in the task itself), or they lead on to the next stage in his design process;

(e) he deems it useful to put into the WS an example of the procedure in his main activity. This indicates to the learners exactly what is required of them, and gives them guidance as to what they might themselves say (in other words he simulates output);

(f) while he does solve a number of issues as they arise, he also shows preparedness to shelve problems that do not find immediate solution. He appears to do this when his design procedure is in full creative swing, and where concentration on a small detail would stem that flow.

George now turns his attention to writing the TN. Once again we shall not here provide a blow by blow account, but will again note that his overall strategy is a methodical one. He starts with the TN introduction, which contains a description of aims, language focus and materials needed. This is followed by a description of each stage of the task. The entire process of TN construction (including the physical process of consigning the notes to paper) takes 31 minutes. Noteworthy in the procedure are the following points:

(a) there are lengthy episodes of philosophising where he considers (for example) at exactly what level to pitch the TN (for experienced or inexperienced teachers, with good or poor English?). Another issue that occupies him is whether teachers should be addressed by direct or indirect speech. Attention to such details reveal George's wealth of experience in the materials design field;

(b)   even at this late stage of TN writing, he shows preparedness to modify the task or add new details to it. For example, he decides to inject a touch of humour by adding 'burglar' to the describee list (thus giving learners the chance to describe the 'ideal burglar'). He also adds a final <u>follow up</u> stage in which chosen pairs of learners repeat their interactions in front of the class;

(c)   almost at the end of his TN writing he decides to add timings to each activity in the task. Noteworthy is the late stage he turns his attention to timing (in comparison with the NS/T designers, for whom timing is sometimes an early and central preoccupation). It is also worth noting that his consideration of timing leads him to abandon various aspects of the task, some of which he spent considerable time agonising over earlier. For example, he deletes several characters from the describee list, after their original inclusion had been the subject of much thought. *It's amazing*, he philosophises, *how normally you end up having to cut things rather than add things*. This 'easy abandonment capacity' is a possible characteristic of good designers;

(d)   as throughout his protocol, George shows plenty of 'task logistics sensitivity'. At one point there is a lengthy excursion into the labelling of items in the WS and TN. He makes sure that the numbers used in the TN correspond to those found on the WS, and in general he puts effort into ensuring that the various means of labelling portions of WS and TN are not confusing to learner or teacher;

(e)   there is again evidence of 'concrete visualisation capacity', associated with <u>simulate</u> codes. For example, he decides to specify in the TN exactly what the teachers should say at various points in the task, and this leads into a lengthy consideration of the language content of the task, accompanied by many <u>simulate input</u> and <u>simulate output</u> codes. As he philosophises: *this, of course, is where you find out whether the task works or not, when you actually try and provide some questions and things for the teacher to ask*.

George now announces that he feels his work is at an end. The researcher/interviewer then asks him a question which she puts to many of our subjects:

> Int: *Terrific. Thank you very much. Have you ever done this task before?*
> George: *No.*
> Int: *I didn't think so. It seemed to be a new creation as it was coming about.*

George: Yes. *I've done that one before, invent a character for a soap opera, which is one reason why I rejected it, although I would have rejected it for the reason I gave. No, I've never done that* [the ideal/least ideal task] *before.*

4.2 An NS/T designer's protocol (D12 – Colin)

Colin is a teacher who at the time of this study is following the MA in Linguistics for ELT programme at the University of Lancaster. The location of his design session is as for George, and the interviewer is the same researcher. Colin has some ten years' experience as a teacher, working in a number of countries in Asia, South America and Europe. Just before coming to Lancaster, he occupied a post of some seniority. At one point during his teaching career, part of his job involved working with a team on the production of tasks for local use. Also, like most teachers, he has throughout his career been involved in modifying published activities for use in a particular contexts. In these ways, Colin is typical of the NS/T group – an experienced teacher and by no means a novice at task design, but without a mass of experience in that activity.

As with George, the interviewer begins by explaining the concurrent verbalisation procedure. She then says: *to get you started and give you practice I have here an anagram . . . I'd like you to think aloud when you're solving it.* Colin solves the anagram in a very short space of time, and is then given the design brief to read. His emotion at the end of this read through is one of relief because the task area covered (describing people) is one that he has dealt with previously in his teaching. He says he knows many textbooks that deal with this function, and he <u>identifies</u> the <u>procedure</u> he will follow, which is to base his task on something that comes from a familiar textbook (from, that is, his existing <u>repertoire</u>). He also announces the intention to start by establishing the general nature of the task he will develop, *and worry about the mechanics of it later*. Establishing the task is a simple matter, because it comes from repertoire. He decides to base it on visuals (the relevant code family here is <u>props</u>). The task framework is that there will be some form of preparation in which visuals will be used to elicit useful language, followed by a main activity in which the learners will use elicited language to describe some new pictures.

This brief discussion (just two minutes long) comprises his *Analyse* stage. There is no *Explore* stage to follow it, and he consequently moves straight into *Instantiate*, where he 'worries about the mechanics'. This is in stark contrast to George, whose *Analyse* and *Explore* stages together last 20 minutes. In this lack of attention to analysis and exploration (particularly the latter), Colin is following the pattern of many NS/T designers, and (as we shall explore in the following chapter) it is indeed the main way in which they differ from the S designer group. Colin works through the stages of his task one by one. The microstages of his *Instantiate* are coded as <u>develop preparation</u>, <u>develop main activity</u>, and <u>develop follow up</u>.

At the first of these microstages, the teacher provides a photograph, and elicits vocabulary from the learners to help them describe what it shows. Important items are written on the blackboard, and mention of this leads Colin to philosophise about the problems of blackboard use in the EFL classroom. Consideration of what to put on the board makes him think a little about the <u>language content</u> of his task, and he identifies areas such as vocabulary, pronunciation and collocation as being worthy of coverage. There is an element of opportunistic planning here as what is essentially a side issue (questions of blackboard use) leads him on almost incidentally to what must be considered a major part of task design – thinking about language content. He then turns his attention to a consideration of the <u>descriptive parameters</u> that will be covered. Under *physical* areas he identifies clothing, facial features and hair. As for *character*, he notes that character description would rely on the describee being known to the learners, and this leads him to suggest that a suitable first stage might be for the learners to describe the teacher: *one thing I've done in the past is get students to describe me first using adjectives*, though he concedes that there might be problems of learner shyness here. Possibly because of this potential problem (though this is not entirely clear) he proposes using description of a famous person as an alternative and mentions a few possible describees – President Clinton, Madonna and Michael Jackson. He then turns his attention to the types of language items likely to occur in description (the language content), checking before he does so that the given learner level is intermediate. He now works through this preparation stage in detail, identifying various sub-stages, noting what the learners and teacher would do at each, and what props would be used. To illustrate the kind of detail that interests him:

> *I usually ask one person to be secretary so they put positive adjectives on one side of their list and negative adjectives on the other side. So obviously that involves considering in groups what the opposites are of each word. Dictionaries could also be used.*

Included in the detail is timing, and he notes that this kind of preparatory vocabulary work could take up to 25 minutes. A state of play statement declares what has been done and what there is to do: *so that's the kind of initial part of the lesson, just to get the vocabulary established. Then we would have to maybe look at the way this vocabulary can be used in sentences.* At this stage he becomes very concrete, considering the actual cases of Michael Jackson and Madonna, and simulating output by rehearsing some of the sentences learners might actually produce. He is also well able to imagine the kinds of issues that will be raised in class: *at this stage inevitably somebody will ask the difference between ... 'she has' and 'she has got',* and he discusses how he would handle this particular problem. Finally in the develop preparation microstage he thinks about timing, and decides that if the activity is to last half an hour overall, he can spend no more than 15 minutes on preparation. He signals his move to the Develop main activity microstage with the words: *and now we need 15 minutes of worthwhile production.*

His first thought about the logistics of this microstage[3] is that the learners should separate themselves out in class so that they are sitting and working alone. Each would choose a class member to be described and, without revealing their choice to anyone, set about preparing their description. But Colin immediately thinks of an alternative, that the teacher herself should nominate the describees by giving out pieces of paper bearing the name of a classmate. He evaluates these alternatives, and decides that the second is preferable because it will ensure that all class members get described, not just the *most dominant, most striking* few. He checks through this procedure, showing a degree of 'task logistics sensitivity' (as well as indicating that the task comes from repertoire) by noting issues such as the following: *I found that if a student says 'how do you say this?', pointing to a spot on the cheek, it automatically gives away the identity of the person they are going to be talking about.* The answer to this problem is for the teacher not to provide too much overt assistance. This section of the microstage ends with Colin identifying his state of play, saying what he has so far done, not just for this microstage but for the task as a whole. Like very many state of play reviews of this sort, this event takes matters forward in some small way – in this case Colin adds some details about the timing of the activities he is planning.

Colin now turns his attention to what happens once the learners have prepared their descriptions. His initial proposal is that they should move round the class describing their chosen person to a number of classmates one by one, up to 15 in all. But he decides that this may lead to tedium, and so modifies the procedure. Rather than simply listening to descriptions, each learner will try to guess who is being described, and will write down the reason for their choice: *what they can do is they can write down 'well student A was obviously talking about student F because he said bla, bla, bla.'* Colin then adds a final stage to the activity, a follow-up in the form of a <u>final plenary</u>, in which selected individuals are asked to read out descriptions to the class. Colin, who throughout is fairly concerned with language content, sees this as a good opportunity to practise reported speech: *people can actually say 'well so and so said that bla, bla, bla' so they're almost, because of the task they're almost obliged to use reported speech without actually having to concentrate on it, which is quite nice.* Finally at this macrostage, Colin expresses satisfaction with his task. He is particularly pleased because it does not involve many materials, a point which clearly has importance for him, since he repeats it later.[4]

Colin now undertakes a short revision of the activity he has designed. This microstage is coded <u>modify task</u>. The first modification comes out of his perception that the task does not require use of many materials. This leads him to begin to enumerate what is required: *it maybe involves one or two photographs of famous people.* He now considers who the describees might be. He concludes that rather than using world-famous characters like Madonna or Clinton, there are reasons to prefer celebrities local to the learners' own country. One advantage is that the teacher might not know these characters, and hence there would be a genuine information gap between learners and teacher. His second modification relates to the final follow-up stage. He suggests that the teacher might practise lexis that has emerged by asking questions about other class members: *the teacher can sort of check understanding by saying 'do you think so and so is selfish, or do you think so and so is shy...'.* Thirdly, he proposes a further follow-up stage – a homework activity which involves letter writing. The macrostage ends with a positive evaluation of the task: *I think I am fairly happy with that. I think it satisfies the criteria. It doesn't involve many materials.*

In the next microstage (coded <u>review task</u>), Colin checks through the task he has designed to make sure it meets the various constraints laid down in the design brief. His check is a thorough one, making mention of a large number of characteristics specified in the brief, including that the group is <u>monolingual</u>, that the learners are adults, at intermediate level, that the language content is used in an <u>authentic</u> way, and that the activity is <u>communicative</u>. His comments are interspersed with philosophising. As throughout the protocol, his philosophising concerns learner preferences, and shows a good degree of 'learner/context sensitivity'. He observes, for example, that learners prefer lessons focusing on vocabulary rather than grammar, and he expresses the view that his task will meet this preference. His one worry is with timing and, like many designers, he feels the activity may take too long. His answer is to propose that the teacher restrict language preparation to a few well-chosen grammatical and lexical points. He discusses at length what these should be, again revealing his concern with the details of language content.

Colin's *Instantiate* stage finishes here, and the remainder of his protocol (some 34 minutes) is spent on *Write TN*. Like most designers, he is reasonably methodological in his approach to this, starting with a <u>TN introduction</u>, stating aims, objectives, materials required, etc., then moving through the task stage by stage. It would be tedious to chronicle this procedure in detail, so (as with George) only salient points will be listed:

(a) as throughout his protocol, Colin makes clear that his procedures follow what he has been trained to do, and what his standard practice is. For example, at the beginning of his *Write TN* he says *so the way I've been taught to write lesson plan is...* Then later: *that's the way I've been trained in teaching...*;

(b) like many designers, Colin uses the *Write TN* macrostage to add new details to the task, and sometimes to modify it, even quite radically. For example, in the course of TN composing he decides it would be a good idea to play some music while the learners are going round class talking to each other, and this detail is duly incorporated. He also works out the homework task in detail, such that at this point one is really speaking of an *Instantiate* procedure;

(c) at one point, the TN writing procedure leads Colin to question his task in a fundamental way, and he philosophises that this is often the case:

> *Right now at this point I'm beginning to have doubts about the task itself, so let's have a bit of a breathing space, but yes I'm just thinking that this often happens that you, in the middle of writing a lesson plan, you begin to have doubts about the task you have already made. This has happened to me before.*

It is not entirely clear from the protocol where his doubts come from (because he does not verbalise it), but it seems to be related to his thoughts on the kind of language content that will be elicited by his task. Having expressed these doubts, he engages in a long process of simulate output, where he imagines what the learners might say when they approach a classmate to ask for a description: *the thing is they can't say 'can I talk to you about, you know Michelle', because the point is they don't want the other person to know who they are talking about, so you have therefore got the problem of whether this activity is authentic or not.* This consideration leads Colin to give thought to the contextualisation of his task, to providing some kind of context which will authenticate the activity. His suggestion is that the learner might be asking about a lost friend. This procedure is a very good example of the benefits of simulate procedures, which here lead to realisation of a rather fundamental shortcoming with the task.

This is very late in the day for the issue of contextualisation to occur to Colin, and it might be seen as a direct result of his failure to consider the overall nature of the task before detailed design begins – a characteristic he shares with a good number of the other NS/T designers. At the same time, it must also be noted that many designers, of the S as well as the NS/T group, do institute changes late in the day, and show a preparedness to make alterations even at points where everything seems firm and decided. This was described earlier as 'easy abandonment capacity', possibly an important characteristic for successful task design;

(d)   again like George, Colin shows a good deal of 'task logistics sensitivity'. For example, when he is talking about ensuring that there is sufficient participation level (with learners talking a lot), he reveals that he has appropriate techniques at his fingertips:

> *There are various ways of ensuring that people speak to more than one person at length. You can clap your hands to make them change or you can pause the music which means they have to change or you can just wander around encouraging them to change after a minute or so. Teachers should be able to do that.*

Unlike with George, we have here not shown any of Colin's action box summaries. In order to indicate the general shape of his design, Figure 4.3 shows the sequence of his macro- and microstages.

4.3   George and Colin: a salient difference

We said at the beginning of this chapter that its main purpose would be to illustrate the kinds of procedures designers follow, and to give some

```
                    Read brief

                    Analyse

                    Instantiate

                           Develop preparation
                           Develop main activity
                           Develop follow up
                           Modify task
                           Review task

                    Write TN

                           Write TN introduction
                           Write TN preparation
                           Write TN main activity
                           Write TN follow up
```

Figure 4.3   Colin's macro- and microstages

indication of how these have been coded. Detailed analysis itself would be saved for the following chapters. But even from this present chapter's basically descriptive account, some differences between the two designers' approaches have emerged. Most salient is the fact that George devotes considerable time to the early *Analyse* and *Explore* macrostages. As a result, by the time he comes to instantiate his task, two issues (among others) have been sorted out. One is that he has a clear idea of the task's purpose – for the learners to describe ideal and least ideal characters. Secondly, he has given the issue of 'causing possible offence to present describees' an airing, and because of this danger decides early on to use a non-present describee. Colin launches far more quickly into designing the stages of his task, thoroughly working out what teachers and learners will do at each point, what language content is likely to occur. But he realises, very late in the day, that the task does not have a true contextualisation, and this he attempts to add rather at the last minute. In addition – and again (one might argue) because he so lacks attention given to analysis and exploring – he has not really aired the 'describee offence' issue, and develops a task which as its main activity has this as an inherent danger – where classmates describe each other.

In Chapter 8 we report on a small-scale evaluation of all our designer tasks, undertaken by a group of teachers. In this evaluation, George's task is rated very highly, and Colin's comes out rather badly. It is possible to account at least partially for the poor rating of Colin's task in terms of what has just been said. Two of the evaluators describe his task as 'confusing' and 'unrealistic', suggesting perhaps that more time should have been spent in considering its overall purpose and contextualisation. Two of the evaluators also pick up on the 'describee offence' issue, and express dislike for the task because it involve learners in describing – and potentially offending – each other.

The degree of attention given to the early macrostages of *Analyse* and *Explore* is an issue discussed in the following chapters, together with other differences between S and NS/T designers, some of which have been suggested in this overview of the entire protocols of two designers.

5
Designing Language Teaching Tasks: Beginnings

This chapter and the next consider task design under three main headings: 'Beginnings' (in this chapter), 'Middles' and 'Ends' (in the next chapter). Each of the three sections begins with a short overview of what typically occurs at the macrostages under consideration, and this is followed by discussion of issues raised at the stages. During these discussions, general points applying to the design process as a whole will be highlighted. So the stage-by-stage organisation is loose, and there are many points at which issues applying to the protocols as a whole are being considered. This chapter will focus on the early stages of task design: the *Read brief* and *Analyse* macrostages.

5.1 What happens at *Read brief* and *Analyse*

This section describes what occurs at the relevant macrostages. Though each heading ('Beginnings', 'Middles' and 'Ends') starts with a descriptive section of this sort, this is longer than the others, partly in order at the beginning to provide a degree of concreteness to the discussion, and partly to provide further familiarisation with the coding procedures followed.

The design protocols always begin with a few minutes of non-design-related talk. The interviewer always asks the designer to talk about himself for a while. The concurrent verbalisation procedure is discussed, and the designer is asked to solve an anagram while talking aloud. Then the design process begins. The interviewer first asks the designer to read the brief aloud. During this *Read brief* stage, some designers see fit to pass comments on what they are reading. Their remarks fall into two broad (and not always easily distinguishable) categories: <u>question brief</u> and <u>comment brief</u>. Sometimes the remarks take the form of questions or speculations.

For example, a designer may speculate on the nationality of the learners, or wonder what is meant by the term 'intermediate'. These are coded as question brief, together with the appropriate referent as 'specification'. So the designer's remark: *OK now what does it mean by adult, it might be from 18 upwards* is coded as question brief: age. The comment brief code is used when a designer expresses surprise (e.g. that the class size is so high), or some other feeling. As we have seen, D12, for example, was worrying about what type of task he would be asked to design, and expresses relief that the required task type is one familiar to him.

Read brief is commonly followed by the *Analyse* macrostage, where the designer checks through the specifications given in the brief, and makes sure he understands what is required of him before any serious designing is undertaken. At this stage the common behaviours are:

- review brief This microstage involves going through the design brief, listing (and often writing down) the component parts – e.g. the class size, the target function required, the level of the learners. As one might expect, the code most commonly found within this reviewing process is comment brief (and, to a far lesser extent question brief).

During the course of this review, or subsequent to it, a designer will often draw attention to particular aspects of the design procedure he is being asked to undertake. There are three codes particularly associated with this:

- identify procedure is where the designer explains how he will go about a particular part of the design (or goes about design in general). Here is an NS/T designer identifying procedure immediately after the brief has been read:

    > *OK right I am going to start off by thinking about the class a little bit. Personally I like them to be working in pairs because I find that is an easy thing to manage...*

    (D13)

- highlight This closely related code is used when a designer highlights a certain point, which may not be a procedure. Here is an S designer stating what he believes a good task should be like:

    > *It has got to be somehow interesting. They have got to be finding out something new about themselves if it is going to have any impact on their minds.*

    (D6)

- <u>identify issue</u> Sometimes highlighted items are expressed in terms of posing a particular problem for task design. More than one designer, for example, notes that real world descriptions of people are often given in monologue form, while the design brief specifically asks for interaction. This is often stated as a problem for the required design activity.

A designer will rarely simply identify essentials or properties. There will also, even at this early stage, be decisions made that are consequent on some of the operations already undertaken. The members of the decision-making family of codes are <u>fix</u>, <u>reject</u> and <u>shelve</u> (like all codes, these are given working definitions in Appendix 1). The *Analyse* stage invariably ends with some kind of <u>fix</u> code, where the designer selects some element that will form the basis for further exploration.

5.2 *Analyse* exemplified: a major difference between S and NS/T designers

It will make the discussion concrete if we give examples of an S and an NS/T *Analyse*. The text of D7's macrostage is too long to be included comfortably, so the action boxes are given instead (Figure 5.1). They reveal many of the features we have mentioned above.

D7's *Analyse* stage lasts five minutes and the transcript is 444 words long. D14's in contrast lasts for just over a minute and is 125 words long:

> OK. So I want character as well as physical appearance and I want them to speak as much as possible but in order to get them to speak I need to give them something to push them to speak, something probably to read or to look at at least. Maybe some pictures and I need to have some sort of reason for them to speak to each other because they're just going to talk. It doesn't really make much sense – they have to sort of interact with each other I think. Ah [reading from brief] 'with as many different members of the class as possible' as well. My first thought is to think of a warmer activity where they perhaps go round and look at each other.
>
> (D14)

This brief look at two *Analyse* macrostages illustrates an important difference between the groups at this point in their design. It is that the NS/T designers' *Analyse* macrostages are considerably shorter than those of the S designers. The averages are: for an S designer 4.65 minutes and for

Analyse

1.
(a)   Fix recipient [*will produce task for published materials*]

---

2. **Review brief**
(a)   Identify state of play: next
(b)   Comment brief: age; monolingual; class hours; level; identify state of play: next
(c)   Comment brief: level; class hours; highlight: practice exercise; fix stage
(d)   Comment brief: skill area; class size; interactivity; comment brief: class size
(e)   Comment brief: activity type; practice exercise; language knowledge; target function; highlight practice exercise

---

3.
(a)   Identify procedure: real world situation
(b)   Identify state of play: doing
(c)   Identify scenario: airport

Figure 5.1   Action boxes for D7's *Analyse*

an NS/T designer just 2.67 minutes. Indeed, the NS/T *Analyse* macrostages are altogether rather meagre affairs. There are the occasional exceptions, and in the section below we shall consider one way in which NS/Ts are as a group more thorough than Ss. But in general NS/Ts do much less before they *Explore* or *Instantiate* than S designers. What is the effect of this on design? As at many points in this study, it is difficult to point to direct consequences. But it seems reasonable to consider the *Analyse* stage to be an important one in task design. If this is the case, then the meagreness of NS/T *Analyse* may be regarded as highly significant.

This issue relates to a point that will become a theme of this chapter and the next, and hence of our entire analysis of task design. It is that the NS/T design protocols show, in relation to the S designers', a 'comparative impoverishment' – a phrase which will recur throughout this chapter and the next. The NS/T protocols are shorter, less rich, encompass fewer variables and consider a smaller number of options. If it is appropriate to describe NS/T design as in some ways 'impoverished', then it is equally appropriate to describe S designer's protocols as 'enriched', and we shall therefore in this chapter and the next also speak about 'comparative enrichment'. A further related term which will occur in these discussions is 'satisficing', a notion mentioned in Chapter 2 and associated with the work of Simon (1981). This is where an individual does the minimum amount of work to get the task done. The result of satisficing will be an impoverished task design procedure.

We therefore conclude that:

> - NS/T designers spend considerably less time at the *Analyse* macrostage than the S designers. This may be seen as contributing to the 'comparative impoverishment' of NS/T designer protocols.

5.3   Questioning and commenting on the brief

What can be said about the question/comment brief behaviour of the designers (at both macrostages – *Read brief* and *Analyse*)? To consider question brief first, Figure 5.2 shows the distribution of these codes. The figure indicates that of the 13 examples of the code, only 3 are from S designers, and the rest from NS/T designers. In addition, the majority of the examples fall within the 'learner and context-related' family (11 of the 13), as opposed to 'task-related' (0 of the 13) or 'design-related' ones (2 of the 13 – one S and one NS/T designer – see Appendix 1 for the codes associated with each of these families). These two observations taken together suggest that (a) the NS/T designers question the brief more than the S designers; and (b) the information felt to be lacking from the brief largely concerns the learners and their context.

The following quotation from an NS/T designer illustrates the sorts of information some teachers feel they need. This teacher asks about length of study, materials used, whether he has been their teacher for long, gender proportion in the group, and language knowledge. As well as indicating what kinds of questions are asked, this example also well shows the extent of the questioning of some NS/T designers. They ask a lot:

> *OK so adults, right. I wonder how long they've been studying for and what kind of materials they have used. I wonder if I've been their teacher before*

Designers	Learner/contextual	Task-related	Design-related	Totals
S	2	0	1	3
NS/T	9	0	1	10
Totals	11	0	2	13

Figure 5.2   Distribution of question brief codes

all of this. – 'you have been teaching', yes. . . . I don't know the composition
of the group, to what extent they are men and women in the group. Let's
assume that they are equal numbers of each, it may not be important
I don't know. Describing people. OK so we've got, they've presumably got
a number of adjectives . . . What is the extent of the adjectives they know?
(D15)

The fact that the NS/Ts seek more information in the area of learner and context-related factors is natural when one considers that their main experience is as teachers and not materials designers. A teacher taking on a new class in a new location (which is in a sense what the design brief simulates), will take pains to establish knowledge of context, to ensure that what he teaches will fit into the local situation. Many of the NS/T designers seem distinctly unhappy (perhaps even insecure) at the lack of sufficient contextual information in the brief – hence their questioning. In contrast, materials writers (most S designers being in this category) cannot cope with too much contextual information, particularly if they are writing for a global audience, in other words for learners working in a great diversity of contexts.

Similar findings relate to the early decision-making of the two groups, in the *Analyse* macrostage (information about this is given in Figure A.4, Appendix 4, and is discussed later in this chapter). By the end of that macrostage, NS/Ts have made slightly more decisions about who their learners are than members of the S group. It is true that some S designers have shown interest in contextual features, but they have wasted little time on making contextual decisions, again doubtless because they are used to dealing with a global audience and cannot take into account the constraints of differing contexts. D6 is a case in point. He laments at some length the gaps in the brief. For example, on reading that the learners are intermediate his comment is: *I would want to know which intermediate* (that is, whether 'intermediate' within a French, Brazilian or whichever other context), while on the question of nationality he says: *we are not told what, which language group these people are in and whether they are Portuguese or Japanese.* Later he sums up his complaints in this area with the comment: *well the information isn't there so I will have to make some sort of compromise. It wouldn't be the first time.* Yet despite these complaints, he ends the *Analyse* stage having taken no decisions at all regarding the learners and their context.

What is being suggested here appears to fit in with the findings of Taylor (1970). He looked at the factors given importance in the planning process of a group of teachers, and also the order in which these factors were considered while planning. The most important factor, and also the one that was attended to at the beginning of the planning process, was the context of teaching. This is precisely the focus that our NS/T designers adopt.

Is this slightly greater NS/T interest in learner and context-related issues continued throughout the design process? The answer is a clear no. To provide some numerical evidence of this, the code of <u>learner action</u> was added to the family of learner and context-related codes, to produce a group of codes showing a feature which might be called 'learning/contextual orientation'. The occurrences of this code group throughout the entire design process were 120 for the S group and just 37 for the NS/Ts. This suggests that overall the S designers show greater interest in these factors than the NS/Ts. Why should this be? It is in fact evidence of a more general characteristic associated with S designers, already briefly mentioned and which we will encounter again in the next chapter. It is simply that, overall, S designers think about more issues, bring more factors into play, than their NS/T counterparts. The S designers' procedure is overall richer, and the greater interest the NS/Ts pay to learner and contextual features (in comparison with S designers) is confined to the early stage of questioning the brief.

Are the same points commented on and questioned by both groups of designers? In general the answer is yes, but the occurrence of two design brief-related codes is worthy of note. <u>Class size</u> is clearly an issue that interest NS/Ts more than Ss (mentions by NS/T designers=4, by S designers=1). The same may be said of <u>time available</u> (mentions by NS/T designers=4, by S designers=0). Both are, one might imagine, high on teachers' agendas when taking on a new class in a new location. We shall consider the question of <u>timing</u> in the next chapter, and will discover that S designers do not ignore this issue at all, but tend to deal with it at a different point.

A further point about the distribution of these codes over the two stages is that the NS/T designers interrupt reading of the brief more than twice as much the S designers (the number of codings for <u>comment/question brief</u> at the *Read brief* stage are NS/Ts=13, Ss=6). The interruptions are also much longer, and as a consequence it takes NS/T designers an average of over half a minute longer than S designers to read the brief from beginning to end. However, if one considers all <u>comment/question brief</u> codings at both stages, it is the Ss who have the higher number – the figures are Ss=56, NS/Ts=47. In other words, Ss overall have more to say and ask about the brief; but they do more of it once the brief has been read. Why should this be so? It is possible that it suggests a lack of systematicity on the part of the NS/T designers, and a preparedness on their part to do more than one thing at once. The S designers read the brief, then make remarks; the NS/T designers often read and make remarks at the same time.

Here are the main points made in this section:

- the NS/Ts question the brief more than the S designers;
- the information felt to be lacking from the brief largely concerns the learners and their context;
- during the design process as a whole, S designers pay greater attention to 'learning/contextual orientation' than NS/Ts;
- Ss read then comment, NS/Ts do both at same time. This may suggest a less systematic approach on the part of NS/Ts.

5.4   Reviewing the brief

At the *Analyse* stage the designer is often occupied in the sensible and beneficial process of what we code as <u>review brief</u>. He is going over the brief, gathering together the pieces of information necessary for the job of task design to be done. Schoenfeld (1985: 297) identifies a number of questions that might be asked of a mathematical problem solver's procedure in the early stages. Two of these questions, which he associates with good practice, are (a) Have all the conditions of the problem been noted? and (b) Has the goal state been correctly noted?

Perhaps similar questions are relevant to the task design domain. Maybe it is reasonable to expect good designers to take note of the various conditions laid down in the design brief, as well as of what is required by way of a final task product. Schoenfeld's 'conditions' and 'goals' are related to our 'learner and context-related codes' and 'task-related codes' respectively.

How efficient are designers at noting conditions and goals? All the S designers bar one (i.e. 7 out of the 8) have a stage coded as <u>review brief</u>. NS/T designers are more varied in this respect; only 3 of them (i.e. 3/8) review the brief in a systematic way. The brief itself includes 15 points that have associated codes (<u>age</u>, <u>class size</u>, <u>target function</u>, etc. – as mentioned on p. 51, there are other brief-related codes which concern points raised in relation to the brief but not mentioned in it). As might be expected, no one designer mentions every single point in his <u>review brief</u>. But seven designers, from both groups taken together, do mention seven or more points, with a good number of designers writing the points on paper for future reference. Although the examples of <u>review</u>

brief in the data vary considerably in length, it may be said that those designers who undertake a <u>review brief</u> do it reasonably well.

But five of the eight NS/T designers do not <u>review brief</u> at all. This lack is a major reason for the shorter length of the NS/T designers' *Analyse* macrostage. Its result is the potentiality for a design procedure which does not fully take into account the various constraints laid down by the design brief. This characteristic may be regarded as a facet of the 'comparative impoverishment' mentioned at the beginning of this chapter.

It is interesting that in a number of the <u>review briefs</u>, as well as points being noted, possible consequences for the task to be designed are also mentioned. We refer to this characteristic as 'consequence identification'. The designer is not just making a list of relevant points, but is beginning to process the mentioned characteristics in terms of task design. So in the following example, the S designer does not simply lament the lack of information about learner nationality; he is also able to articulate a number of consequences of this lack of knowledge for task design:

> *There is a genuine problem of not knowing whether we are dealing with Pacific rim members. . . . How much can I assume what they may already have done in vocabulary? . . . Japanese intermediate level is in reality quite different from European intermediate level. Are there any clues from this brief which help me to clear that point? It would also be useful to know that because we know that they are monolingual and it is in their country.* [Reading brief] *'Communicative activity', so the culture therefore also would have some bearing on whether they are likely to want to communicate, I mean at times you can't stop them communicating. You want the learners to interact as much as possible – are they learners who come from a culture where this sort of interaction requires something heavy and difficult . . . ?*
>
> (D6)

In the example above it is the consequences of a lack of a piece of information that concerns the designer. The following example illustrates how a piece of information in the brief leads to an immediate decision regarding the nature of the task to be designed:

> *You want the members to interact as much as possible with as many different members of the class as possible. OK so it has to be something that is getting them up and moving them round a little bit.*
>
> (D11)

Though D11 is an NS/T designer, there are slightly more examples of S designers following up consequences in this way. It might be regarded as a hallmark of good design practice.

In summary:

- those who review the brief do so in an efficient way, but five out of the eight NS/Ts do not do it at all.
- some designers immediately think through the consequences for task design of points raised even at this early stage. Consequence identification may be considered efficient design practice.

5.5   Identifying perspectives, frameworks and important considerations

Schoenfeld (1985: 295) argues that early in the design process (he has an *Analyse* stage which is roughly the same as ours) the good mathematical problem solver will 'introduce important considerations' and 'select perspectives and frameworks for working a problem'. These processes are for him aspects of metacognition (what he calls 'control'). Perhaps we can expect similar behaviour from the good task designer. The relevant codes here are identify procedure and highlight. Before considering designers' behaviour in relation to these codes, we need to note that these concepts are sometimes difficult to identify in the data. A designer may mention a number of considerations regarded as important at any given stage, and the analyst often has to make difficult judgements as to how 'central' these are in the designer's mind, and whether they truly constitute 'selecting a perspective', as opposed to just making a passing comment. Note also that at present we are considering what designers *say* they will do, and what they *say* they find important. We shall later consider evidence that they do not always do what they say they will.

Figure 5.3 lists considerations designers raise at the *Analyse* stage, under relevant samples of identify procedure and highlight. A piece of terminology in this figure: we refer to 'taskifying'. 'Taskification' is defined in Appendix 1 as the 'procedure of thinking of a real world situation and converting it into a task fit for class use'. More than one designer identifies this as an important design procedure.

Two points emerge from the figure. One is that all the S designers (D1–8) make some comment about perspective, framework or important considerations, while only three of the NS/T designers (D10–17) do so. This

Designer	Procedures identified and characteristics highlighted
D1	Think about task type
	Think about a task genre
D2	Task should have differential distribution of information (task genre)
	Identify real world situations in which people are described
	Taskifying
D3	Provide some motivation for learners to speak
	Identify real world situations in which people are described
D4	Think first about who learners are
	Then identify real world situations in which people are described
D5	Task should have differential distribution of information (task genre)
D6	Task must be interesting and self-revelatory (task type)
D7	Identify real world situations in which people are described
D8	Identify real world situations in which people are described
	Taskifying
D10	None
D11	Task should involve learners moving around class (task type)
D12	None
D13	Task should have differential distribution of information (task genre)
	Identify real world situations in which people are described
	Think about who learners are
D14	Provide some motivation for learners to speak
D15	None
D16	None
D17	None

Figure 5.3 Perspectives, frameworks and important considerations raised at the *Analyse* stage

provides some of evidence in support of the notion that experienced designers do indeed identify perspectives, frameworks and important considerations early in the design process. It also provides a small amount of further evidence of 'comparative impoverishment' in the NS/Ts' design procedures. If identifying procedures and highlighting are, as Schoenfeld suggests, important, then the NS/Ts' comparative lack of it is impoverishing.

Secondly, it is interesting to note the considerable variety from designer to designer in terms of perceived approaches to design. The figures in Figure 5.4 clarify how often the items mentioned in Figure 5.3 occur. This conclusion is potentially important because the presence of such variety suggests the need for care when making prescriptive statements about best practice in task design. There are clearly various possible

Identify real world situations in which people are described	6 (5 S + 1 NS/T)
Think about task genre	4 (3 S + 1 NS/T)
Think about task type	3 (2 S + 1 NS/T)
Think about who learners are	2 (1 S + 1 NS/T)
Provide some motivation for learners to speak	2 (1 S + 1 NS/T)
Taskifying	2 (1 S + 1 NS/T)

Figure 5.4 Number of times the procedures and characteristics in Figure 5.3 are mentioned

starting points to task design, with (as yet) no evidence that any one approach is better than any other. This is particularly interesting in the light of what was found at Stage 1 of the ESRC study, briefly described in Chapter 1. There, the participating designers were interviewed regarding their language teaching beliefs. As I note in Johnson (2000: 313):

> One of the findings at that stage was that there is a basic grounding of similarity, a shared basis, to all the designers in the study. All associate themselves in various ways with so-called 'communicative language teaching', and claim that they strive to be 'communicative' teachers. It follows from this that all are likely to have been trained in a similar way, will have read the same background books, have been exposed to the same ideas, and to an extent share the same preoccupations.

But this shared perspective is clearly sufficiently broad a church to permit differences of approach within it. Despite designer similarities, there are distinct differences in the way that they tackle design. This finding is reminiscent of Clark & Yinger's (1979) one, mentioned in Chapter 2, that individual teachers do differ in terms of planning style.

This section has suggested that:

- S designers identify procedures and highlight more than NS/Ts. These codes may be associated with Schoenfeld's 'identifying perspectives, frameworks, and important considerations'
- the NS/T designers' comparative lack of these codes may again suggest 'comparative impoverishment'
- there is considerable variety from designer to designer in terms of perceived approaches to design

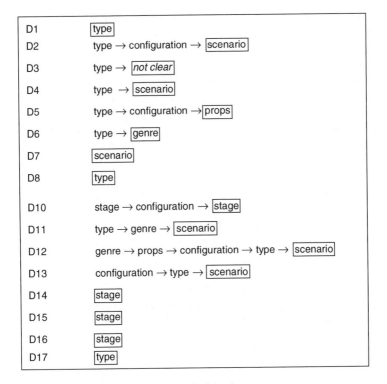

Figure 5.5   Some decisions made by end of *Analyse*

5.6   What decisions are made

We noted earlier (p. 75) that 'the *Analyse* stage invariably ends with some kind of <u>fix</u> code, where the designer selects some element that will form the basis for further exploration'. What exactly has been fixed by the end of the *Analyse* stage, and are there differences between S and NS/T designers in this respect? Full details of the designers' decision-making at the *Analyse* macrostage, together with their reasons, are given in Figure A.4 in Appendix 4. Figure 5.5 focuses on selected details of what has been fixed by the end of the macrostage. The items are listed in the order in which they are decided upon, and the codes appearing in boxes indicate those decisions which lead designers directly into the next design stage, whether it be *Explore* or *Instantiate*.

It is possible to divide the codes appearing in this figure into three categories according to degree of abstractness. At the most abstract level (let us call it Level 1) are <u>type</u> and <u>genre</u> which deal with families of tasks identified in terms of shared characteristics (e.g. tasks that involve a lot of moving round the class, or tasks containing an information gap). At Level 2, a more concrete level, comes scenario. A scenario may be regarded as an exemplar of a particular task type or genre. Codes associated with Level 3 are configuration, props and stage. These deal with more concrete, even 'mechanical' aspects of tasks.

In terms of these levels, Figure 5.5 reveals two things. One is that NS/Ts have more Level 3 codes than S designers, the figures being 8 and 3 respectively. Stage is, in particular, an early preoccupation with some NS/T designers. This code refers to the planning of the stages the task will eventually have. A number of NS/T designers begin mapping out stages this early in the operation. D15 provides an example. Initially in his short *Analyse* he gives attention to contextual properties. Then he thinks about what language the learners will want to practise further ('adjectives', he decides). This is immediately followed by planning of the first stage of his task:

> *OK yes so I think adjectives are the, most important thing ... Perhaps some kind of activity before this activity just to bring these things that I presume they have covered to mind just to refresh memory. So perhaps some activity to elicit ... the adjective structures that they know already, some kind of brainstorming thing. ...*

> (D15)

The early NS/T preoccupation with stage relates to an issue discussed in Johnson (2000). I suggest there that some NS/T designers' attempts at task design are in fact the drawing up of lesson plans. The difference between creating a task and devising a lesson plan is that the latter will often (though not necessarily always) base itself on some already existing, given series of activities (appearing in a textbook for example). Level 1 and 2 decisions have usually already been taken before the lesson plan is drawn up. That plan will focus attention on Level 3 – the 'mechanics' of the operation – showing concern for the description of stages, procedures involved, possible class configurations, questions of timing.

As Figure 5.5 shows, stage is not the only Level 3 code represented in NS/Ts' early planning. Below is the whole of D13's *Analyse*. It is far from being a poor *Analyse*, and compares favourably with D14's given earlier in this chapter; it thus serves as a useful reminder that NS/Ts must not be treated as straw men. D13 does discuss 'high-order' issues. What is relevant here is that in the midst of discussion about the procedure of selecting from <u>repertoire</u>, and about an appropriate <u>genre</u> (the use of an information gap activity), a decision is made about the 'mechanical' issue of <u>configuration</u> – he decides to use pairwork:

> *OK so my first thought is definitely I will be thinking about something I have already done in the past. I am going to base the activity on something I have done or possibly . . . an amalgam of things that I have seen from bits and bobs from different books. OK right I am going to start off by thinking about the class a little bit. Personally I like them to be working in pairs because I find that is an easy thing to manage but I also I don't mind mixing activities. But I actually like pairwork because I think people can work, be at different levels within pairwork so I am probably going to do a pairwork activity from that angle. And I have got to think up a way of getting some kind of information gap, which is going to use the language of describing people. In other words where one person is describing someone possibly and the other has to find out information about the person. But I want to try and put it into some kind of situation which is relevant to them or at least has a real life world type situation which they might conceivably use the language in. So something I have used in the past has been a missing person, where if we look at, it will be a role play situation OK.*

(D13)

The second point which Figure 5.5 reveals is concerned with the relationship between higher- and lower-level decisions. Although S designers do make Level 3 decisions, these always follow a decision about a higher-level issue – specifically, what task <u>type</u> or <u>genre</u> will be used. The same is not true for the NS/T group. In the case of D15, for example, his identification of the first stage of his task is in fact the beginning of his *Instantiate*. Figure 5.5 shows that half the NS/T designers (four out of eight – D10, 14 and 16 along with D15) do just this,[1] while none of the S designers use the identification of a stage as the launch pad into *Explore* or *Instantiate*. What is particularly significant about D15's procedure is that he moves straight into detailed design of his task's first stage without having much idea at all about what the task as a whole will look like. There is no attention given to overview. He, together with the other three NS/T designers mentioned, seems to be moving to the design of parts when the shape of the whole has not been fully conceived.[2]

Figure 5.5 shows that a common procedure for designers other than the four who go straight for <u>stage</u> is to make more abstract decisions before more concrete ones. For example, D2, D4, D11, D12 and D13 move from <u>type</u> to <u>scenario</u>. That is, they make decisions about general task type before they decide on specific realisations of that type. Other designers do not show any progression in the *Analyse* macrostage. D1, D8 and D17, for example, leave the macrostage with decisions about <u>type</u> and nothing else. But at least this is a Level 1 code, and Level 2 decisions about <u>scenario</u> follow later, in the *Explore* or *Instantiate* macrostages. We may therefore say that all these designers follow an 'abstract → concrete' sequence in their design. So, to continue with the example of D2: his first decision is that he will use an exercise type that involves 'differential information' – different members of the class being given different pieces of information (as in 'information gap' and 'jigsaw' activities). After some time considering what configuration to use (he decides on groupwork), he fixes on a scenario – a game in which class members have to identify each other. This decision about <u>scenario</u> leads him into the *Explore* stage (where, with time, he moves on to other scenarios).

It is important not to exaggerate the use of an 'abstract → concrete' sequence in those designers other than the four who go straight to <u>stage</u>. None of the designers in our study follows a sequence that might be regarded as entirely 'logical' or systematic from beginning to end. They all take short cuts, show elements of opportunism, and make lower-level decisions while supposedly concentrating on higher-level ones. We should not therefore be surprised to see, in Figure 5.5, that D5 makes an early decision on two Level 3 issues: <u>configuration</u> and <u>props</u>, and that it is indeed the latter that carries him forward into his next macrostage. Nevertheless, designing parts before the whole does seem associated with some NS/Ts, and we need to ask what its effect is likely to be. In theory there are two possible results. One is that the whole will never really be planned, and the eventual task will lack coherence. The second is that the 'whole' will be planned late in the day. This is likely to be inefficient in design terms because it may result in the necessity for massive redesign; it will also possibly result in a task that is weak in conception and imagination (commodities being brought into play late in the day), though elegant perhaps in logistics (to which so much attention has been given).

As an example of late higher-level planning we may cite D12, whose protocol was examined in detail in Chapter 4. Towards the end of his design procedure, he becomes worried about the inauthenticity of his language content. This consideration leads him, as we said in Chapter 4, 'to give thought to the contextualisation of his task, to providing some kind of context which will authenticate the activity. His suggestion is that the learner might be asking about a lost friend. . . . This is very late in the day for the issue of contextualisation to occur to D12, and it might be seen as a direct result of his failure to consider the overall nature of the task before detailed design begins. . . . '

This discussion on the use of strategies such as 'abstract → concrete' needs to be tempered by the expectation that it is not reasonable to expect every decision made to be articulated by the designer. A major reason for lack of articulation will be the use of repertoire – when the designer bases his task on an already existing one. Where this happens, the designer will be importing a task type/genre and a scenario, without a great deal of discussion. The result may then appear to be a 'messy' development, apparently missing in essential items, which are assumed rather than discussed by the designer. The use of repertoire is a major issue, which will make several appearances in this chapter and the next – and will reappear again in Chapter 7.

This section has suggested that:

- NS/T designers tend to focus on concrete considerations early in the design process. This is particularly true with regard to the planning of <u>stages</u>. One way of viewing NS/T design is as the creation of lesson plans;
- S designers, and a number of NS/T designers, follow an 'abstract → concrete' sequence in the consideration of task features. But a significant number of NS/Ts do not do this, and can be accused of giving no attention to overview. This may be seen as leading to later design problems.

5.7   Do designers do what they say they will do?

In Chapter 2 we discussed the literature on teacher planning, noting that according to studies by Taylor (1970) and Zahorik (1975) and others, teachers often depart in their planning from the generally accepted algorithm they have been trained to follow. Is the same true in task design? The question is difficult to answer because there is apparently no such generally accepted model of task/materials design, and indeed the applied linguistics literature has remarkably little to say on the topic of design procedures. Nunan (1989: 137) does have a section labelled 'Creating tasks', and this contains a few comments on the sequence of procedures to be followed in task design, but these go little beyond the statement that 'the starting point for task design should be the goals and objectives which are set out in the syllabus or curriculum guidelines which underpin your teaching programme' (p. 137). He then says that 'the next step is selecting or creating input for learners to work with'. Hutchinson & Waters (1987) view things from a slightly different perspective, and have as their first stage the selection of a suitable text for teaching purposes. Monitoring language content in terms of syllabus does occur, but at a later stage.

Neither of these sources (nor others consulted) throws much light on how task designers might be expected to behave in relation to a task design activity such as the one given to our subjects. It might make an interesting research project to ask a separate group of subjects to articulate what they would regard as a sensible way of attacking the exercise; that is, they would be asked, not to design the task, but to say how they would go about designing it. This might provide some information about whether a generally accepted procedural sequence exists in people's minds, if not in the literature. We could then compare expectations with what actually happened.

But our data do provide some evidence in this area. No less than half of the S designers in the study state that they are going to start by attempting to identify real world situations in which *describing people* would be the natural thing to do. The following four quotations, each from a different designer, all come immediately after the design brief has been read (and, in some cases, one or two characteristics of the design situation have been commented on):

I may just think of a setting, a scenario of some sort where describing people is going to be a necessary or a plausible thing to do. I think that's the starting point – to try and find some, some context where describing people is going to be necessary.

(D7)

Right, well several things occurred to me as I was reading this and I wonder if I can retrieve what those thoughts were. Yes the describing people thing I started to think of, well what are the circumstances under which we describe people? In other words are there sort of real life applications of this which would give a, set in a context, a purpose, a need for the exchange of information and so on?

(D2)

Right so the starting point really needs to be a natural situation in which describing people would actually occur.

(D8)

So I have to think now of a situation where these adult learners and I'm going to say that they're sort of middle class well I could really cheat and say they're middle class Swedes or but or shall we say mixed Europeans, oh they're monolingual they can't be mixed. Of mixed variety of ages. And when would you actually describe people. Only when you're meeting some-body I suppose or you want to identify somebody at a party . . .

(D4)

These quotations suggest that in the eyes of at least half the S designers there exists a belief that task design should begin with the identification of real world situations in which the function to be practised occurs. One of these situations would then be 'taskified' – converted, that is, into a classroom activity.

But is this what the designers do? In all cases the answer is a qualified no, and sometimes the contrast between stated strategy and actual practice is immediate and startling. Hence the sentence which follows D7's above is:

Yeh I'm actually thinking back and thinking through to some of the stuff that I've done and some material I just wrote. I had some people meeting, meeting visitors at an airport and instead of having to have the people they were going to meet described to them yeh that was quite good though I'm not quite sure how we'd do that with 15 to 20.

(D7)

The same is true in all other cases where the stated intention is to explore real world situations. It does not in fact happen. This example also suggests the role that repertoire plays in task design, a topic devel-oped in the next section.

There are a number of reasons why the 'no' is a qualified one. Firstly, there may be a sense in which D7 has considered real world situations. What is happening is that he is taking from repertoire a task he has seen, used or developed at some earlier point in his experience. That task may well have been developed following a fuller consideration of real world situations. In this case the work of considering the real world has already been done, and all that remains is to take the task wholesale from repertoire. In Johnson (2000) I use the phrase 'repertoires as short cuts' to describe this procedure.

A further qualification relates to the nature of the *describing people* function. One designer in particular, D8, is insistent that he would like to follow a strategy which has as its first stage the identification of real world situations, and he repeats this wish several times at different stages in his design process. His preferred overall strategy would continue with the process of 'taskification'. But (like some others) D8 laments the fact that exemplars of real world descriptions of people are few on the ground; the functional area is not, in other words, amenable to the strategy he would normally employ. He expresses his frustration at this on more than one occasion. Here is an example:

> *So not so easy to think of the natural situations that would work with a group like this, where this kind of language would arise naturally and would need to be used. There must be such a situation, there must be, there must be more than one of them in fact. Let's see now . . .*

(D8)

So the failure to put stated strategy into practice may to an extent have been brought about by the particularities of the functional area being dealt with in this case.

In conclusion:

> - there is some evidence for recognition of a general design strategy which involves initial identification of appropriate real world situations exemplifying the target function, and then 'taskifying' one of these;
> - designers do not always follow this strategy, even when they say they will. One reason for this may be related to the specific function under consideration; some designers find it difficult to think of real world 'describing people' situations.

5.8 What designers in fact do

As we have just seen, D7 does not continue to explore real world situations, because he thinks of a task he has developed before which contains the *describing people* function. Once the designers have completed their tasks, the interviewer always engages them in conversation, seeking their informal views on the task they have just designed. In very many cases (but unfortunately not all) they are asked whether

they have designed the same or a similar task before; Chapter 4 illustrates D1 being asked this question. The answers to the question therefore provide information about the extent to which the designers
draw on repertoire when selecting a task, taking it from the 'bank'
they have drawn up through experience. Added to this source of information are instances of the code <u>repertoire</u>, used during the design
process itself when designers volunteer the information that a task or
procedure comes from repertoire. In this latter case, and where the
reference to repertoire relates to the task as a whole, it is mentioned in
the final (shaded) column in Figure A.4, Appendix 4. From these
sources it becomes clear that repertoire is an important source of
inspiration for our designers, particularly when it comes to the major
process of selecting a task for development. Taken together, the
sources show that no fewer than 4 of the S designers and 6 of the NS/T
group – 10 out of the total of 16 designers – admit that their tasks
originate from repertoire.

Here are three quotations illustrating how designers acknowledge
repertoire as a source. In the third, the designer explicitly states that his
task design strategy in general involves early search in repertoire:

*Also when I first saw describing people I immediately think of other pub-
lished materials I am familiar with so it is not going to be something I do
from scratch. I can draw on those materials for ideas and for information
gap activities or something like that.*

(D12)

*OK what I am thinking about now, actually is I am thinking of some of the
tasks that I have done in the past already and I have got one particular one
in mind that I might want to use.*

(D13)

*I guess I am going to try put together ideas that I have already used in some
new way or put together ideas that I have seen in books, in resources elsewhere, and combine them in my own way. That's how I usually do these
sort of things. And maybe something new and revolutionary will turn up in
the process.*

(D16)

It is perhaps natural to think of borrowing from repertoire as in some
sense a reprehensible procedure – a means of satisficing. From this

point of view, it would be gratifying to be able to paint a picture in which NS/Ts are found to use repertoire in a major way, with S designers avoiding its use and planning tasks as if from scratch. But such a view would conflict with findings, discussed in Chapter 2, in which expertise is seen as a question of specialised knowledge possession. According to that view, experts possess a larger repertoire than novices, and use it accordingly. It is the novices who are forced to design from scratch, because they do not have sufficient repertoire to enable them to avoid this mentally taxing procedure.

Developing a coherent stance towards use of repertoire will form a major part of Chapter 7. Here it needs to be said that although in our data NS/Ts do use repertoire a little more than Ss, it is by no means the case that S designers avoid its use. The coherent stance cannot therefore be built on the assumption that repertoire use is an NS/T phenomenon. The picture is more complex than that.

Another point which emerges as we look at how designers make decisions is that it is sometimes 'opportunistic' – a notion introduced in Chapter 2. Here are two examples. One concerns D2 and the pathway that leads him to decide on a groupwork configuration. The first thing he decides on is a task type – one which involves the 'differential' deployment of information round the class (as in information gap and jigsaw activities). This leads him into a consideration of scenarios, the first of which involves the class working as a whole (a type of configuration). He rejects this scenario, but out of this consideration comes a decision regarding configuration – to use groupwork. This decision is as it were incidentally made through reflection on one particular scenario and its associated configuration. The second example relates to D12's protocol, one of the two we considered in detail in Chapter 4. In his *Instantiate* phase he decides on a task which involves a preparation stage at which learners have to describe a famous person. His positive evaluation of this task lies in the fact that it does not require too many materials – just a few photos. This evaluative consideration leads him to think about who the photos might be of – about describees, that is. At this point he alights on the idea that it might be useful to have a describee who is famous in the learners' country, but who might not be known to the teacher. Although he has expressed worries about his task being too long, this idea leads him to propose a new stage for his activity: learners will first describe a universally famous person. Then they will describe to the teacher a locally famous person. This new stage comes about from an evaluation of his task in terms of props.

This section has suggested that:

- repertoire is an important source of inspiration for designers. Taking from repertoire cannot be regarded as reprehensible satisficing, and is by no means exclusive to the NS/T group;
- designers, both S and NS/T, provide examples of opportunistic designing.

5.9   The emerging picture

During the course of this chapter on the beginnings of task design, several tendencies have emerged in association with the two designer groups, Ss and NS/Ts. The cautious word 'tendencies' is used because in some cases the differences are little more than that. These emerging tendencies are grouped around two themes. The first is the theme of 'comparative impoverishment'. We find that although the NS/T group question the brief more, and seem insecure with the lack of contextual information it contains, in general they do 'less' rather than 'more' in several important ways. As regards the beginnings of task design, this impoverishment is wholly associated with a reduced (or completely lacking) *Analyse* macrostage. This results in impoverished review brief microstages, and less attention (than the S designers give) to identifying perspectives, frameworks and important considerations. There is also, in the protocols as a whole, less overall interest in learning/contextual factors.

The second theme is associated with early attention to logistical (Level 3) issues during design, which in some cases leads to developing the details of a task before its general shape has been established. We have suggested that one way of conceptualising this tendency is to say that some NS/T designers are developing lesson plans rather than tasks.

In order to state matters in a positive light, we may say that the more experienced S designers show the opposite tendencies. So their design procedures are comparatively enriched, with more elaborate *Analyse* stages, more attention to reviewing the brief, identifying perspectives, frameworks and important considerations, and more overall interest in learning/contextual factors. They also show a healthy early concern with establishing the overall shape of tasks before embarking on details. We shall find that these emerging themes continue as we now turn to the later stages of task design.

6
Designing Language Teaching Tasks: Middles and Ends

6.1 Middles: the *Explore* macrostage

6.1.1 What happens at *Explore*

What do designers do at the *Explore* macrostage? The short answer is that they consider various possible options for a task, focusing on particular genres, or scenarios, or task types or frameworks. The chief operators related to the consideration of these options are: identify, consider, propose, develop, compare, evaluate, reject, modify, review, with the stage usually ending with a final fix. Designers also identify and solve issues as they come across them. As their procedures require, they may check the brief on occasions, and codes such as philosophise, and identify state of play occur throughout.

Figure 6.1 illustrates the kinds of activity undertaken at the *Explore* macrostage. It shows a summary of an S designer's action boxes.[1] The figure indicates that the designer considers a number of real world situations as candidates for the basis of her task. At the end of her consideration of each, she shelves (rather than abandons) them – until (g) at least. In (f) she returns to the situation she first considered, and divides it into two versions – A(i) and A(ii). After due thought she shelves A(i) and abandons A(ii). She then returns to situation C, which she finally selects.

As with the *Analyse* macrostage, there is an important point to be made about the occurrence of *Explore*. All but two of the S designers (6 out of 8) explore, but only two of the NS/T designers (2 out of 8) have this macrostage at all. In the case of these two, their macrostage averages just 7 minutes in comparison with the average length of the S designer's *Explore* which is 14 minutes.

The procedure exemplified in Figure 6.1 is therefore very much one associated with the S designers. The characteristic approach of NS/T

Explore
(a) Identify real world situation A
(b) Identify real world situation B; explore; shelve
(c) Identify real world situation C; explore C; shelve
(d) Identify real world situation D; explore; shelve
(e) Identify real world situation E; explore; shelve
(f) Reconsider real world situation A; identify real world situation A(i); explore; shelve
(g) Identify real world situation A(ii); explore; abandon
(h) Reconsider real world situation C; fix

Figure 6.1 Summary of an S designer's *Explore* action boxes (pilot data)

designers is in dramatic contrast. They alight very quickly (at the end of their *Analyse*) on a task type which will serve their purpose. They then spend the major part of their time instantiating. Or (as we began to see in the previous chapter) they simply begin instantiating without really alighting on a task type at all, and hence lack a clear view of what the task as a whole will be like. We may regard this lack of an *Explore* macrostage as a further example of comparative impoverishment of the NS/T designers' procedures. This will be illustrated in the following sections in relation to some specific procedures.

6.1.2 Breadth first and depth first processing

The NS/T lack of attention to the *Explore* stage is related to various differences between the design procedures of the two groups. One of these concerns the breadth first (BF) versus depth first (DF) strategies mentioned in Chapter 2. As general strategies of problem solving, BF or DF procedures will be evident at many points during the design process. We shall here concentrate only on the main process of arriving at a final task, considering how the designers proceed from their start to that point at which they have identified the task that is to become their final choice, the beginning of the *Instantiate* macrostage. If we focus on this main process, it is the case that the S designers in our study predominantly use a BF approach, while NS/Ts are overall DF. Figure 6.1 is a clear example of a BF strategy; if situations A(i) and A(ii) are counted separately, then the designer considers six different possibilities before selecting which one to take forward (though as we shall see in the following paragraph her treatment of one possibility is in depth). D6 provides a further example. His *Explore* considers five possible genres and scenarios. He evaluates and rejects the first four, then decides on the fifth. The times spent on considering each possibility are rather evenly distributed: 7 minutes for possibility 1, 5 for possibility 2, 7 for possibility 3, 6 for possibility 4 and 5 for possibility 5.

What Figure 6.1 does not show is the amount of time the designer spent on each event. They in fact all last a few minutes only, until (g) is reached. She then spends a whole hour on exploration of situation A(ii) before abandoning it. This suggests two things. Firstly, although she adopts a predominantly BF strategy, this does not save her from the necessity to do some in-depth designing, which as it happens turns out to be a blind alley. As an approach, this makes good sense; however cautious a designer might be in considering a variety of task possibilities, at some point the bullet has to be bitten and detailed designing commenced. The calculation is that the exploration of various possibilities will have eliminated the least hopeful candidate tasks, and that – in Bereiter & Scardamalia's (1993: 58) phrase – a 'judgment of promisingness' will have led to fruitful choice of a task for in-depth development. But the possibility of dead ends can never be eliminated even by the most experienced designers.

Secondly, it is noteworthy that this designer is able, ready and willing to abandon a possibility even though such an amount of time and effort has been put into it. We saw a further example of this in Chapter 4, where D1 dropped a number of describees from his list, late in the day after much attention had been given to their inclusion. We referred to this as 'easy abandonment capacity'. Two further points may be made about this capacity. One is that although taking tasks from repertoire is both a normal and a sensible strategy, it can also have behind it a reluctance to abandon something already worked out. This is possibly present in D12's protocol. He takes a task from repertoire, and although it becomes clear towards the end of the design process that the task does not meet the constraints of the design brief (it concentrates for example on physical description and does not cover character description), he does not abandon it. Secondly, it is important that a designer who abandons confidently should not lower her guard and fail to undertake essential filtering out of unpromising tasks by means of a BF strategy. Here is D3 expressing his own lack of 'easy abandonment capacity'. In so doing he is signalling how important it is for him to use a BF strategy and not commit himself to a task for development until he is sure that it is entirely suitable:

> *I see that by this stage I've got firmly committed to this task and I've no interest whatever in pursuing it. But to abandon it means a whole lot more work, and I don't want to do it, I want to make this one work . . . the*

last thing I want is to back off from what seems to me a fertile idea because I think the earlier stage is quite painful, the business of floating around in a void trying to get something that'll work. Once you've got hold of something there's a tremendous surge forward and you don't want to get off that road. It's very hard abandoning something and starting again.

(D3)

We have given two examples of the BF strategy at work, but the point needs to be emphasised that it is an overall characteristic of S and not NS/T designers. To a large extent (though not entirely, because events at the *Analyse* stage can have relevance) one can recognise the presence of a BF strategy by the existence of the *Explore* macrostage. As the working definition in Appendix 1 states it, *Explore* is the stage at which the designer 'considers various possible options for tasks, before finally alighting on one'. The NS/T designers' lack of *Explore* is therefore closely connected to adoption of a DF strategy.

From sections 6.1.1 and 6.1.2 we may therefore conclude that:

- many NS/T designers miss out the *Explore* macrostage altogether, and when it does occur it is rather short. NS/Ts tend to alight quickly on a task type which they immediately begin to instantiate;
- in contrast, S designers *explore* at some length. Lengthy exploration is highly related to the use of a BF strategy, which is predominantly followed by S designers.

6.1.3   Enrichment: choice creation and self-imposed complexification

The small (or more often non-existent) amount of time NS/T designers spend on *Explore* in comparison with S designers exemplifies a further difference between the two groups which becomes apparent at this macrostage, though it applies the protocols as a whole. It is that S designers tend to evoke and consider alternatives in any given situation. This applies when they are considering selection of a task, which is why they tend to include sometimes quite lengthy *Explore* stages, at which alternatives are considered, evaluated and a final choice made. But it also applies at lower levels – where for example selection of a configuration type is being considered. While the S designer will typically talk through several possible configurations, there is a tendency for the NS/T designers to think of one configuration, and immediately go with that. The presence of two further codes signals this characteristic of 'choice creation'. One is <u>alternative</u>. This occurs 16 times in S designer protocols, and only 3 in NS/T designers'.[2] The second code is <u>reject</u>, because it implies that more than one possibility has been (or is about to be) considered. We find four times as many instances of this code in S designer protocols than in those of the NS/T group.

Figure 6.1 provides a good example of choice creation at work. Here the designer shows she is prepared to consider a good number of task possibilities before making her choice. To illustrate choice creation at some macrostage other than *Explore*, here is D4 during her *Instantiate*. She is trying to decide how learners will be provided with information about the person they are to describe:

> D4:   *So how on earth am I going to get them to do that? The next thing I've got to decide is what will the input be, what is going to carry the language. Is it going to be spoken input, or written? It could be an email, something like that which is half written half spoken language. It could be a tape recording input and I've got to try and get them to talk. All right. It would be dreadfully boring to write it I think. What would you do? You could send an email to somebody and that could be the language work. You could give everybody a photograph I suppose. Just running through possibilities here. You could have a visual input, it would have to be full length photograph or pikky of some sort. You give it to Group A and they have to either describe or email somebody or write down, or telephone a description of that person and then you'd have, the pictures would perhaps parade through and they had to plan how they were going to meet her or him. OK Have I got any financial constraints on this?*
>
> Int: *Only if you wish to introduce them?*
>
> D4:   *Right OK. Well I think what might be fun would be to use bits of video maybe. Video clips, that would be hard to organise in class because they're going to have to watch them individually. I wonder if they could do that? That would be great fun. I'm not sure that it's feasible from a management point of view. So that's my other constraint then.*

The management constraint she mentions in fact eventually leads her to drop the video idea. The referent code used in relation to this extract is <u>input carrier</u>. D4 here considers three types of input carrier – spoken, written and visual. The actual carriers that are considered are email, tape recording, photo and video. Note how she pursues each possibility a little in order to explore its feasibility. In some cases she makes evaluative comments.

D4's consideration of input carrier is detailed and quite rich. It is difficult to contrast it fairly with an NS/T designer, in a way that does not invite accusations of selective exemplification. But if we stay with the same referent, input carrier, we find that there are 8 examples of the code in the data set, and 7 out of these occur in the S designer protocols. This in itself suggests a degree of comparative S designer enrichment of the type we shall discuss later in this chapter under the name of 'maximum variable control'. Here, to stand as a comparison with D4's treatment of input carrier, is the one NS/T designer reference to the matter:

> *OK. What materials would I need? I think tape, and I'd need to make sure that they've all seen a film, but if they haven't seen a film, supposing I was somewhere that they didn't have access to films or they weren't interested in films it would have to be something. But there are always stories if you didn't have films I suppose you could use fairy stories, or folk tales or something.*

(D14)

It is true that D14 does consider an alternative (films versus a story). But note how short the discussion is. Note also that D4 was *just running through possibilities here*; that is, she was considering alternatives in order to provide a selection. D14 on the other hand considers alternatives in case films should not be available or appealing in her context. It is 'what to do if something is unavailable or unappealing', rather than 'what possible ways are there of providing input'.

Choice creation may be seen as part of a more general process of 'complexification'. This in turn might be conceptualised as the opposite of 'satisficing', a process mentioned at various points in earlier chapters. One area in which complexification is particularly evident throughout the protocols relates to the code identify issue. Satisficing will presumably result in avoidance of any issue that may make the task design process more complex than it needs to be, while the protocols of designers who seek to enrich their tasks are likely to be high in identify issue codes. The numbers cannot be said to suggest that the NS/T designers satisfice – there are 52 NS/T identify issue codes. But there are 82 instances for S designers, and this does indicate that S designers do indeed complexify. Reading through the protocols as a whole, one is left with a further impression: that often S designers' tasks could be developed satisfactorily without these complexities. Complexification seems to be a self-imposed burden, a strategy to enhance enrichment and avoid satisficing.

The S designer D7 may be taken as an example. There are 18 <u>identify issue</u> codes in his protocol. One of his chief concerns is <u>language content</u>, and he spends more time than most thinking about the appropriate language for input to learners and output from them. Below are a few of the issues he raises in relation to <u>language content</u>. It is difficult to illustrate the 'self-imposed' nature of complexifications, but these particular examples have been chosen to suggest that what is being dealt with are issues that enrich the task but may be regarded as not central to it, in the sense that the task could go ahead without these issues being addressed:

- he is unhappy about establishing language content without the help of data. He suggests referring to a corpus which might provide firm evidence of how speakers do in fact describe people;
- he is equally unhappy that some of his language content is not 'generative' in the sense of being usable in many contexts. He seeks to introduce language which is highly transferable, and hence of maximum use;
- he is concerned to find (and stimulate practice in) sequences of functions. So he wishes to avoid single statements like *He's a very serious person*, and seeks to join them with relates sentences to form sequences like *He doesn't laugh very much, he's a very serious person.*
- the language content he plans is, he notes, rather male oriented. He raises the issue of introducing some female describees to redress the balance;
- he worries a lot about what words to introduce, and shows great cultural sensitivity in this area. For example, he is nervous about the word 'workaholic' because of associations with the term 'alcoholic' – a culturally dangerous notion in some contexts. He is also concerned about use of the word 'partner' as opposed to 'spouse', because it can imply a practice of cohabitation that would not be acceptable in some cultures.

Self-imposed complexification is particularly interesting in the case of D7 because (as we saw earlier) he is one of the designers who takes his task from repertoire. He has designed the task before, and hence presumably already thought about language content. But this previous treatment does not stop him from considering the issue again. Like many S designers, D7 is 'making life more difficult for himself than it needs to be'. A read through the description of D1's design procedure in Chapter 4 leaves the same impression. He is constantly discovering issues which make simple design an impossibility. Or is 'discovering' the right word? Perhaps 'inventing' better captures the spirit of self-imposition; he invents issues.

As with input carrier (considered earlier in this section), it is difficult to contrast D7's treatment without appearing to engage in selective exemplification. If we stay with the language content code, we once again find many more instances of the code for S designers (49) than for NS/Ts (18), again suggesting the enrichment/impoverishment theme. But these instances do vary very much in length, and interest in the language content issue does differ considerably from designer to designer – a question discussed later in this chapter. Below, in their entirety, are the language content references of D15 – an NS/T designer. The amount of attention he pays to this topic is roughly average for the NS/T group. Also characteristic of that group is the focus on concrete details of actual exponents to be introduced. Note also how in the last quotation below, D15 (again characteristically) thinks about language content in relation to the specific mechanics of how the teamwork will operate. In fact D15 does not consider language content in terms of problematical 'issues' at all. Unlike D7, he is simply developing language content, and the coding identify issue: language content would not be appropriate an any of the instances below:

...or we could use structures even like you know – 'What's his name?' 'How old is he?' 'Where does he live?' 'What does he do?', sort of various bio-data leading onto describing that person, 'What's he doing?' 'What's he wearing?' 'Who does he look like?' or 'What does he look like?' So perhaps eliciting those kind of structures, likes dislikes.

(D15)

OK what else might we want to use. OK describe physical appearance, character. OK yes so I think adjectives are the most important thing.

(D15)

Another possibility is that they don't describe but that the other members of the team ask questions so they will say things like – 'Is she tall?' 'Is it a man is a woman?' 'Is she tall?'...An easy version is a kind of an open question, OK so the open question is basically a Wh-question. So – 'What is she wearing?' which would require the person whose go it is to say quite a bit but would require the other people in the group at least to form a first question. So – 'What is she wearing?' 'What does she look like?' 'What's her name?' 'Where does she live?', perhaps that kind of thing.

(D15)

Thus:

> - S designers tend to evoke and consider alternatives in any given situation;
> - 'choice creation' may be seen as part of a more general process, associated with S designers, of complexification. The process might be described as being 'self-imposed' in the sense that acceptable, less rich, versions of the task might be developed without them.

6.1.4   Control (metacognition)

As we saw in Chapter 2, Schoenfeld finds more evidence of 'control' (metacognition) in his experts than in his novices. The codes in our system associated with control are evaluate (and codes like reject which signal the results of an evaluative process), state of play, highlight, identify procedure, and possibly also philosophise.

The creation of choices, which we discussed in the previous section, automatically implies the use of evaluation, to arbitrate between choices. We noted in that section that S designers create more choices that NS/Ts. We would therefore expect to find more S designer evaluations, and we have already seen that the group have more reject codes than NS/Ts. The numbers do indeed show that the S designers engage in more evaluation than NS/T designers; the figures are 67 instances of evaluate codes for S designers, and 49 for NS/Ts.

One of the designers who evaluates the most is D1, whose protocol was described at length in Chapter 4. Below is a substantial quotation from that protocol, beginning at the point at which he suggests including descriptions of 'least ideal' as well as 'most ideal' describees in his task. As we saw in Chapter 4, having decided on that, he goes on first to consider – and reject – a possible alternative task (the 'genetic engineering' scenario). He then begins to draw up a list of possible describees. Notice that in the case of almost all of the many alternatives he considers throughout this extract, there is an <u>evaluate</u>, followed by a <u>reject</u> or a <u>maintain</u>:

> *That would give more variety, more range of things but at the same time would also I think be more fun as well because describing what you don't like is often much more interesting and would probably be funnier than describing what you really do like.* So that's what I'd be going for, it would be something like that. That would be essentially what we would be doing – describing ideal or least ideal. *It would depend also on the context. If we wanted to give it a more intellectual context, we might think of it in terms of ideas about genetic engineering where you need to go along to the sperm bank and set down the requirements that you want for the father of the child. I suppose we would have to keep it sort of gender neutral . . . but I think that's probably making it a bit too complicated, a bit more complicated than it needs to be, although it might be fun in some situations.* So we're describing these sorts of people, ideal or least ideal. *We're going to need a few examples, the one I've got down is [writing] ideal or least ideal and we've got boy friend/girlfriend or husband/wife. Then we might have something like doctor, bank manager although doctor and bank manager might be fairly similar in a way. Presumably most people would say they would want a sympathetic and one who knew what he was talking about and so on, so we may get a bit of redundancy in that. They might not be too interested in that. What other kinds of people might you interact with and have a view as to what they were like? Teacher is the obvious one although that could be a bit dodgy depending on whether they start to describe the actual teacher they've got as the least ideal but assuming people wouldn't do that. Friend, your best friend would be another one you could have. I would be tempted also to put parent . . . but I think in some societies that might be a bit of a no-no. Respect for parents and so on is very strong in parts of the world.* So you've got boyfriend, girlfriend, husband, wife, doctor, teacher, best friend . . . *Ah how about pilot, airline pilot . . . probably not a very good one actually.* So you've got best friend, film star, yes.

> (D1)

Another characteristic of D1's designing which is illustrated by this lengthy extract is that following a good number of evaluations there is an explicit statement of what has been decided, indicated by use of another code associated with control: <u>state of play</u>. Examples of <u>state of play</u> are marked in the extract above by the use of non-italics. The figures for use of <u>state of play</u> throughout all the protocols are 42 for S designers and 18 for NS/Ts.

As we saw in Chapter 2, Schoenfeld's experts regularly use something akin to our <u>state of play</u>. He exemplifies with the protocol of one expert which, he says, shows that 'a monitor-assessor-manager was always close at hand during the solution attempt. Rarely did more than a minute pass without there being some clear indication that the entire solution process was being watched and controlled, both at local and global levels' (1985: 310). The same may be said about D1 (the designer with the most occurrences of <u>state of play</u> in our data) and some others in the S group. With some designers the sequence *propose alternative* → *evaluate* → *state of play* → *'move on'* is so common as to be considered as a strategy. This sequence is well illustrated in the extract from D1's protocol given above. For example, he introduces the genetic engineering idea (<u>propose alternative</u>), decides it is too complex (<u>evaluate</u>), returns to the 'ideal/least ideal' scenario (<u>state of play</u>), and begins to consider potential describees (moving on).

As the phrase 'move on' in the previous paragraph suggests, it is natural that states of play should act as transition markers for the end of micro- and macrostages, signalling movement from one topic to another. The designer states what has been done before moving on, or considers what is to be done next before doing it. This function is well revealed in the action box summaries. Figure 6.2 shows D8 writing his

---

5. *Write WS*
(a) Identify state of play: next; identify title; describe TN aim
(b) Describe activity; identify state of play: done, next
(c) Identify issue; identify issue; consider describee; fix cards
(d) Fix describee type; consider data collection; consider describee type
(e) Identify issue; identify state of play: done

---

6. *Write TN*
(a) Identify state of play: next; describe purpose
(b) Consider alternative task; reject
(c) Describe activity; identify issue; review describee; review language content

---

Figure 6.2   Action box summaries of D8's *Write TN* and *Write WS*

TN and WS, with each line in the summary roughly equivalent to a microstage. There are four mentions of <u>state of play</u>. Note that they all come at the beginnings or ends of lines in the summary, showing their transitional function. The junctions between macrostages are particularly major, and D8 finishes one (*Write WS*) with an <u>identify state of play: done</u>, immediately beginning the next (*Write TN*) with an <u>identify state of play: next</u>. The purpose of <u>state of play</u> from the designer's point of view is that it enables her to keep track of exactly where she is in the design procedure. It reminds her not only of what has been done and what is left to do, but also what is being done. This last is important to ensure that she does not get lost in the maze of issues which must occupy her mind at any given moment and are potential threats to coherence.

The protocols are full of examples of designing in which the direction changes often, where issues are partially dealt with and then left, and where diversions lead off in unpromising directions. To provide complete evidence of this would be lengthy. But consider this brief episode in the protocol of D11. At the point where the quotation below occurs she is deeply involved in planning her main activity, which is a role play based on a 'detective asking for description of criminal' scenario. She is working out in detail what the learners will do at each moment during this activity. Then she says:

> *And also what am I going to be doing while they are doing the task? So I thought of say maybe if I spend about 10 minutes reviewing the adjectives first, and then maybe about 5 minutes setting the scene, maybe with a picture or something to set the scene like a robbery or something and just elicit some vocabulary from that.*
>
> (D11)

So the issue of what the teacher will be doing during the main activity leads her to think about preparatory stages at which the teacher's role will be clearer. It takes her a while to extricate herself from this diversion. D11 is one of the designers with the least number of <u>state of play</u> statements, and her protocol is characterised by diversions and failure to see topics through to their conclusion. One might like to think that more expressions of <u>state of play</u> might have helped her. But it does need to be remembered that such expressions are not in themselves necessarily of much use; it is possible for a designer constantly to be signalling what she has done, is doing, is about to do. But these signals may be quite inaccurate, and need not in themselves display coherent design; the presence of coherence markers is, lamentably, not necessarily a guarantee of coherence.[3]

Of the other codes associated with control, <u>highlight</u> and <u>identify procedure</u> were dealt with in Chapter 5 as they relate to the early stages of design. Uses of the code <u>philosophise</u> provide some interesting insights into design procedures, and Appendix 5 contains selected pieces of philosophy (as well as instances of <u>identify procedure</u>) which throw some fascinating light on the thought processes of designers. But the actual occurrences of <u>philosophise</u> (and the points at which they occur) do not perhaps tell us very much except how helpful a designer wishes to be to the researchers. One imagines that the thoughts they express would not be articulated during naturalistic design.[4] Some of the designers – particularly the professional textbook writers – were delighted that at last research was being done into their design processes, and this doubtless led some of them into copious <u>philosophise</u> episodes!

The important conclusions related to control are:

- there are more instances of <u>evaluate</u> codes in the protocols of S designers, a characteristic that can be related to S designer choice creation;
- S designers also use <u>state of play</u> a lot. This regularly serves as a transition marker, and helps designers keep track of the position reached and avoid getting lost in a morass of detail. Some designers seem to follow a sequence of *propose alternative → evaluate → state of play → 'move on'*

6.1.5   Important issues raised in section 6.1

There have been two main themes in this section. One is a continuation of the impoverishment/enrichment motif. The S designers, with their longer *Explore* macrostages, their choice creation and their complexification (often self-imposed), add a richness to their design procedures lacking in the NS/T group. The second theme is control. This was an issue touched on in Chapter 5 where we saw that the S designers identify more perspectives, frameworks and important considerations. We have now seen that they also evaluate more and have more state of plays than NS/T designers.

6.2   Ends: the *Instantiate, Write TN* and *Write WS* macrostages

6.2.1   What happens at *Instantiate, Write TN* and *Write WS*

At the *Instantiate* stage, the designer puts meat onto the skeleton constructed in the previous macrostages. The favoured procedure is for designers to go through their task stage by stage in the order in which they are done by learners (that is, *preparatory stage(s) → main activity → follow-up activity*). But some designers prefer to plan the main activity first; it is, after all, usually an idea for the main activity alone that starts off the *Instantiate* stage. Preparatory and follow-up stages are then added. After each <u>develop stage</u> there is often a <u>review stage</u>, sometimes followed by a <u>modify stage</u>. A final <u>review task</u> (possibly accompanied by <u>modify task</u>) characteristically leads into the *Write TN* and *Write WS* macrostages. Alternatively, the <u>review stage</u> may appear after the TN and WS have been written.

In order to illustrate what characteristically happens as a task stage is constructed, Figure 6.3 shows a summary of some action boxes in D5's protocol. It is taken from the beginning of his *Instantiate*, where he is developing the preparatory stage of his task, a 'find the difference' activity. To make the summary comprehensible, some explanatory notes have been added on the right. As this figure shows, during the development of individual task stages the whole gamut of parameters associated with task construction arise. Among the most common referents for *Instantiate* (and indeed *Write TN* and *WS*) are: <u>activity</u>, <u>learner action</u>, <u>props</u>, <u>describee</u>, <u>language content</u>, <u>configuration</u>, <u>teacher action</u>, <u>timing</u>.

Many designers treat the *Write TN* and *Write WS* macrostages as a second pass at *Instantiate*, going through the design of their task in more detail, and adding more specifics to it. The activities that occur at these *Write* macrostages are therefore more or less the same as for the *Instantiate* macrostage. TN and WS writing are activities at which the <u>modify</u> code occurs frequently, as designers descend into detail and thereby are confronted with points that need changing.

6.2.2   Taking the stages together

The point has already been made that a good deal of instantiating work goes on at the *Write TN* and *Write WS* stages, and indeed in some cases it is entirely through TN and WS construction that instantiation takes place. In effect some designers do most of their detailed task design through the process of writing worksheets and teachers' notes.

3. *Develop Stage 1 (demonstration)*

(a)	Identify props: photos; identify issue[1]	1. How many photos should there be, and what size?
(b)	Consider describee; check brief;[2] identify descriptive parameter;[3] identify issue[4] fix describee[5]	2. To see how old learners are, the class gender proportion, what language they know already; 3. Decides to include dress as a parameter; 4. What is the ethnicity of the learners – to help decide on appropriate describee; 5. White Caucasian
(c)	Describe stage: prerequisites;[6] teacher action, learner action; identify issue;[7] modify stage[8]	6. Things that will be needed in class, like blue tack; 7. How many photos will be needed?; modify stage; 8. Cuts down on number of photos
(d)	Identify stage: revision; describee;[9] identify issue;[10] modify stage;[11] identify issue;[12] review stage[13]	9. Of language already known, describing a classmate; 10. Touchiness issue involved in describing classmate; 11. To leave it up to teachers whether classmates are described; 12. If publication is required, pictures could be used at this stage; 13. In terms of aim and describee
(e)	Develop stage: language content; review stage[14]	14. In terms of activity and props
(f)	Identify describee[15]	15. Considers different describee types for different groups
(g)	Identify stage: feedback;[16] philosophise[17]	16. On work just done; 17. Says he is designing a lesson rather than a piece of material

Figure 6.3 Summary of some action boxes from D5's *Instantiate*

The reason why TN/WS writing is so helpful in instantiation is presumably because in task design so much of the devil really is in the detail. A number of designers philosophise along these lines. As D3 puts it:

> *Now I'm just writing out instructions for doing this as I would write them out for a teacher and hoping that this will show up any weak links or things that aren't, things that wouldn't work.*

It is only when the kind of detail required by TNs or WSs is confronted that issues and problems, particularly logistical ones, arise.

It is possible that some language educators (assuming they had anything to say on the matter), might recommend a task design model in which the ideal sequence is: design the task in its entirety, then set about writing TNs for it. Such ideal(istic!) types of model do indeed surface in other areas of language education. Some for example believe that syllabus design should precede materials design, such that a syllabus should be drawn up in full before any teaching materials are produced. One can understand the justifications for such 'logical' and 'systematic' sequences. But are they followed in practice? Though there are in our study task design who do follow the *design task → write TN/WS* sequence, there are also many who do not. Since so much devil is in the detail, those who do not cannot be condemned.

Given these deliberations, we shall in this section deal with *Instantiate* and *Write TN/WS* together.

6.2.3   Cyclic design

Clark & Yinger (1979) study five teachers preparing their lessons. They find that their teachers' planning is not linear but cyclical, moving from general idea through a series of elaborations. As we have already implied, task designers can show a degree of cyclic design as they return to issues at the *Write TN/WS* macrostages, and add details to what has already been designed during *Instantiate*. But many designers follow a cyclic design process more generally than this, revisiting issues time and time again not just across macrostages, but also within the same macrostage. Often cyclic design is a clear strategy, with the following stages:

- designer creates the outline of a task;
- she reviews this outline;
- during the course of this review, or following it, some new detail is added to the outline;
- because the new detail has led to a revised (and more detailed) outline, this sparks off a fresh review which in turn leads to a new detail.

Here is an example of how a review leads to addition of some new detail. It comes from D7's *Instantiate*. At this point he is reviewing what has been decided about his preparatory stage. The decisions relate to language content. But as part of that review he makes a 'new' decision about the teacher's role during it:

> *so we'd have a focus in the initial phase, in the preparation phase we'd focus on the language and we'd make sure through some activities that they've got a language focus and that they're sort of confident and have plenty of chance to practise. And during that phase, during this preparation phase that's where the teacher is going to have to monitor very closely what's going on.*
>
> (D7)

This 'new' detail about the teacher's role accordingly becomes part of the task, and makes an appearance in further reviews which follow.

Here is a more extended example of how designers undertake several 'passes' through a task design, modifying and developing as they go. It is taken from D11's *Instantiate*:

'Passes' 1, 2.   Her task begins life as a genre – role play – to which she attaches a scenario: the fairly popular one (among designers) of a detective interviewing witnesses to a crime, eliciting descriptions of the criminal. This is 'Pass 1' at which the decisions made concern genre, scenario and learner roles. In Pass 2 (which soon follows) she adds a configuration – learners will work in triads. She also decides on props/ input carrier – a photo of the suspect – and sketches out language content for both the detective and the witnesses.

'Pass' 3.   Throughout her designing, D11 places emphasis on ensuring that all the participants in her task should be occupied all the time. She now identifies a very practical issue, concerned with the learners: what will Witness 2 do while the detective and Witness 1 are interacting? This issue leads her to the conclusion that it will be better for the learners to work in pairs rather than triads, with one detective and just one witness. Pass 3 therefore begins with a modification of the configuration, changing it to pairwork. As she then reviews what will happen in the new configuration, it occurs to her that using many photos of different possible suspects (rather than just one) will increase the interest of the task. She therefore modifies her props to be a number of photos – she eventually fixes on six. Having this number of photos available leads her to consider a further sophistication. She now decides to have learners swapping roles (the code is <u>role swapping</u>), taking it in turns to be detective and witness.

'Pass' 4.   True to her concern that all participants should be occupied all the time, she now asks herself what the teacher will be doing while

this activity is going on. She decides that the teacher will be insuffi-ciently engaged, and this leads her to a lengthy consideration (described earlier in this chapter, on p. 107) of the task framework as a whole. She decides that there will be a preparation stage at which the teacher will provide input. She works out the timing for this stage and for the main role play activity.

'Pass' 5. D11 now develops the plan she has devised. What each learner will do is now specified in greater detail than before (looking at photos, thinking of questions, and so on). Each of these constituent activities is assigned a timing. A teacher action for the main activity is now fixed, involving <u>facilitating</u> and checking against L1 use (coded <u>TL check</u>). As she reviews the learner actions and mentions the idea of role swapping, it occurs to her that learners might also move round the class, changing pairs (being a detective with one partner and a witness with another).

The example well illustrates how considerations of detail lead to task modifications. It also suggests the important role reviewing plays in this process. Task design involves near 'simultaneous planning' (the phrase, used in an entirely different context, is Halliday's – 1970: 145); a large number of variables have to be juggled with at the same time. It is all too easy for a designer to become bogged down in consideration of one variable, losing track of the whole. Some designers insure against this is by constant reviewing. Their rule seems to be: *if anything changes, go back through what has been decided to establish how things now stand.*

The example above from D11's protocol contains reviews, and in the protocols of others there are even fuller ones, which go over every single detail so far established, and are undertaken at regular, frequent intervals. Our data also include examples of design where so many modifications to a task are added, without controlling reviews, that the track is lost. In one case, a kind of meltdown occurs and the researcher/ interviewer has to intervene and assist with design (by questioning), to clarify how the task works.

A further advantage of cyclic design, accompanied by reviews whenever change is made, is that it allows an 'even descent into detail'. If too much consideration is given early on to any one design variable, it can exert too controlling an influence over the task as a whole. For example, if <u>configuration</u> is worked out in great detail before other important aspects of a task (e.g. learner action, language content) have been established, then the designer is condemned to working his task around an elaborately specified configuration, possibly to the task's detriment. Working on all variables to a roughly even degree, then adding further levels of detail, ensures more even development.

We have seen above how review can act as an important 'change instigator code', leading to modifications and developments in a task. Identify issue can play a similar role, and this is exemplified in Figure 6.1, given earlier in this chapter. The figure contains five examples of the identify issue code and all lead, directly or indirectly, to change. So in Figure 6.1's stage (c) the issue of how many photos will be needed leads to a modify stage, while introduction of the 'touchiness issue' in (d) leads to an addition to the TN. This designer is thinking of (or creating, or even inventing) issues, the solutions to which lead to task modifications or developments.

To summarise sections 6.2.1–6.2.3:

- many designers use *Write TN* and *WS* as a way of continuing to instantiate their task, in a cyclic fashion; indeed, much of the instantiation may occur at these stages;
- *Write TN* and *WS* may therefore be seen as part of a cyclic design pattern. There is also more general evidence of cyclic design in the protocols;
- in cyclic episodes, the review process plays an important part. It is often the instigator of change, leading to modifications or the addition of detail;
- cyclic design has the advantage of ensuring 'even descent into detail', where designers work on many variables to a roughly even degree.

6.2.4   Concrete visualisation capacity

In Chapter 4 we spoke (with reference to D1's protocol) of a characteristic which we named 'concrete visualisation capacity' – the ability to envisage possible classroom activities in great detail. We suggested that this characteristic might be important for good design.

One way in which concrete visualisation is both manifested and put to use is through the practice of simulating. Simulate codes occur in many protocols of both S and NS/T designers – the frequencies of occurrence are not significantly different for the two groups. Simulate is where the designer imagines the actual words used by teacher (simulate input) or learner (simulate output). The value of simulating is partly that it forces the designer into a useful degree of detail, revealing issues that need facing and problems that need solving. In the example below, D8 has proposed a 'Twenty Questions' type of guessing game. He now overtly states that he will begin instantiation by talking through an example of what learners might say during the game. In the course of exploring this example by means of a <u>simulate output</u>, he identifies an issue associated with having a group of people (e.g. the Spice Girls) as describe, rather than single individuals. The simulation also leads him to decide that questions should be restricted to the yes/no type:

So let's just take an example. If they were asked, supposing the person in question was ... someone these people know, Michael Jackson. May be not Michael Jackson, the Spice Girls. 'Are they male?' 'Is he male or female? Female'. Right then, sooner or later they're going to find out that. 'Is she?' How may be you can't really use the Spice Girls, 'Is she?' How would the student answer that? He would want to correct them and say 'not she, they', alas yes unfortunately. ... Anyway so got to think of another famous person that these people are likely to have some knowledge of, ... Let's take a religious leader, let's take the Pope. 'Is he young?' 'Is he old?' 'Is he brilliant?' 'Is he married?' 'What is he?' 'Does he?', 'Does he live in?' So it's got to be yes/no questions. ... 'Does he work in a bank?' The other players ask yes/no questions to find out. The player with the card answers 'yes' or 'no' ... or 'I don't know'. Yes, OK.

(D8)

<u>Simulate input</u> can act as a kind of rehearsal for a teacher as to what she will say during the class (even though the intention is of course that the designed task should be used by someone else). Some designers leave the impression that they are simulating input as a kind of security measure, to give them the peace of mind that detailed rehearsal brings. Here is D10 simulating how she will tell learners to describe a person. The use of 'I' in the first sentence reveals that she is indeed thinking about her own teaching, not that of anyone else. This piece of <u>simulate input</u> focuses the designer's attention on the issue of <u>describee</u>, which she then pursues:

But I'll say to them 'Just choose someone you know well it could be anyone, it could be your boss, it could be someone who you manage at work, it could be your child if you want to, or, yes but it's got to be some-body, it needs to be someone you know really well ... '. And they don't need photos although obviously if you can give people a bit of notice and get them to bring in photos that's a nice idea but that's not always possible especially if someone just picks up the activity at the last minute.

(D10)

One may hypothesise that one major determinant of degree of 'concrete visualisation capacity' relates to the degree of domain knowledge and the size of the repertoire that a designer possesses. These are also reflected in the speed and ease with which concrete details are brought to mind. Earlier in this chapter we saw how D4 considered various possible input carriers, and in the process of considering each was able very rapidly to provide sketchy details of the scenarios these input carriers might occur in. The lengthy quotation on p. 100 itself exemplifies this, and the way that it continues provides further exemplification. Here is how she continues her consideration of video clips as a possible input carrier:

OK ideally my first fun thought would be to have 3 or 4 video clips of real people, fairly distinctive people I suppose and similar ones to them as decoys, coming through, just walking through a corridor or something. Maybe one could even get a clip out of a film, I don't know, which Group A would select or be given to describe. Group B would be given one to describe, Group C etc. or however many we're dividing our class into and they have to either write an email or, yes I think we're going to make them write an email to somebody about it. Then we all watch the video.

(D4)

D4 is able to visualise what would need to be in the clips, and how the class would use them. She does this very quickly, and in some detail. It is also being done for just one of a number of possibilities she considers, and indeed within a few sentences she rejects the input carrier with the words: *OK this has got to be in a textbook, so goodbye television. What a shame.* Here concrete visualisation capacity enables her to consider a number of possibilities very quickly but to such a degree of detail that proper evaluation of each possibility can take place. A useful skill indeed.

Thus:

- designers display 'concrete visualisation capacity'. One manifestation of this is in <u>simulate</u> codes. Simulating both input and output allows detailed consideration of class procedures, and can lead to task modifications;
- the ability to sketch out candidate procedures in a rapid but detailed way allows them to be evaluated in a swift but thorough fashion.

6.2.5   Maximum variable control

A theme of this study has been the comparative richness of S designers' design in comparison with that of NS/Ts. S designer protocols seem to include 'more of everything'. This reflects itself in the occurrences of codings throughout the protocols, and seems to lead to tasks which are designed taking into account a large number of variables and constraints. The overall occurrences of all codes in all S designer protocols number 788, while for NS/Ts the figure is 483. This gross figure does not tell us much, and we need to look more closely at individual code occurrences to appreciate the comparative richness of S designers' work. We therefore made a selection of codes relating to task content. We were interested to know whether considerations like 'gender' or 'outcome' (to choose but two) are given equal attention by the two groups. The occurrences of each code (over the protocols as a whole, not just the *Instantiate/Write WS/TN* macrostages) were then counted. The numbers are given in Figure 6.4. In each case they are higher for the S designer group.

   We shall here follow up just two items from this list. The figures for the two groups relating to gender/gender proportion in Figure 6.4 are neither high nor particularly dramatic – four S designer occurrences as opposed to one NS/T. As the working definitions in Appendix 1 clarify, gender proportion relates to the number of males/females in the class, and is a design brief related code. There are only two occurrences of this

Code	S designers	NS/T designers
Descriptive parameter	24	5
Gender/gender proportion	4	1
Input carrier	7	1
Language content	49	18
Learner action	47	9
Outcome	13	1
Purpose	5	0
Teacher action?	36	9

Figure 6.4   Occurrences of selected 'task content' codes in S and NS/T designer protocols

code in the data, one in an S and one in an NS/T protocol (D5 and D15). D15 wants to know, at the <u>review brief</u> microstage, how many males and females there are in the class, and D5 checks whether the brief has anything to say on this matter at the beginning of his *Instantiate*. But when it comes to actually designing his task, D15 does not refer to the gender proportion factor at all. Despite what he asks at the <u>review brief</u> microstage, his design is simply not sensitive to gender considerations, and the same holds true of all NS/T designers. The only occurrences of the <u>gender</u> code (defined as 'ensuring equality of gender treatment') are in the S designer protocols. In the case of D5, he follows up his check of the brief with a statement that his language content will reflect the gender factor:

> OK so I would have maybe men and women mixed up in this particular group. Then go through them, decide partly on the basis of what I've been able to get [in the way of visual props] what sorts of vocabulary and language is going to be appropriate for describing them again trying to make sure there's a reasonable spread of physical characteristics amongst the people so that you've got male/female, young/old.

> (D5)

D7, on the other hand, has not commented on male/female proportion at the <u>read brief</u> microstage, but during task construction he shows sensitivity towards the factor:

> I think we need to bring some women into this because all the phrases that I noted so far start with 'he', so we need to start with 'she': 'She's quite tall', and 'He's not very tall'.

> (D7)

Similarly, D8 notes that all his describees are men, and adds some women. So although the instances of the <u>gender</u> code are few, we may say that it is a variable that some S designers (but no NS/Ts) cater for.

The <u>descriptive parameter</u> code provides a second example. As Figure 6.4 shows, over the protocols as a whole there are 24 mentions by S designers and only 5 for the NS/Ts. There is also considerable difference in the length of these occurrences. In all, 5 of the S designers discuss <u>descriptive parameter</u>, spending an average of 5.1 minutes on the topic. Just 3 of the NS/T designers consider this matter, and spend an average of only 2.6 minutes on it. D13's coverage is average for the NS/T group. He is devising a 'description of criminal' task and has reached the point in his *Instantiate* where he is working on logistical details:

> *if it was say somebody ringing up the police station the policeman could actually write down ... it would be better if they had a checklist or something so we can have something like a tick box with height, colour of eyes, colour of hair, build, clothes and what else do we want in? Personality, smoke, 'Does he smoke?' Right OK.*

> (D13)

Note that this consideration of <u>descriptive parameter</u> occurs almost incidentally, and within the context of logistical planning. D13 is looking for 'contents of his tick box' rather than undertaking a survey of possible descriptive parameters.[5]

S designers pay much more attention to <u>descriptive parameter</u> than this, and indeed two of them develop tasks where the factor is worked into the task's fabric. Learners are divided into groups, each of which concentrates on a different <u>descriptive parameter</u>. These two designers in particular spend a good deal of time in arriving at the right number of parameters. Here is one of them:

> *So you get groups of, 5 groups, and they construct questions. The first group, Group 1 constructs questions on colour, line. Group 1. Group 2 constructs questions on, yes this is quite fun, on movement, on the way the people move like 'Do they walk fast or do they walk slowly?' or whatever. Group 3 – yes it is vital that it covers the main modalities. The visual and the audio, so Group 3 could work on description of voice. Group 4 could work up questions on the look of faces and Group 5 could work on something else, it could go beyond the physical perhaps. All that's physical, well it is not really but it just seems physical. We have covered visual and kinaesthetic there. Smell is important but too delicate. Group 5 could look at X, I am not sure what.*

> (D6)

Examples such as the two given suggest the presence of a factor which we might call 'maximum variable control'. S designers produce tasks that are sensitive to more variables, take into account more factors. It is a central feature of the comparative enrichment which S designer protocols possess.

We therefore conclude that:

> • S designers develop tasks which take into account more factors than those of NS/Ts.

6.2.6   Language versus task orientation

In Chapter 5 we noted that the subjects used in this study shared a basic grounding in communicative language teaching, and all aspired to be 'communicative teachers'. We also noted that it is to be expected that within this general pattern, there should be differences between designers. Perhaps the most major one, which seems to occur across the S–NS/T divide, is between *language-oriented* and *task-oriented* designers.

We have already suggested (on p. 103) that S designers as a group show more concern for language content than NS/Ts. But within each group there are differences of approach between individuals suggesting a language or a task orientation. D7 is the best example of a 'language-oriented' designer. As we have seen, he spends a good part of his design time considering the linguistic output associated both with the real-life *describing people* situations he identifies, and (more) with the task he develops. There are no fewer than 18 occurrences of the <u>language content</u> code in his protocol, and on p. 102 we listed some of the language content issues he identifies as important. The example below illustrates the degree of detail he goes into:

> *so we might look at things like 'He's quite tall', 'He's not very tall' which I think is much better than saying 'He's short', to say 'He's not very tall', that's much more . . . 'He's quite tall', 'He's not very tall'. 'He's quite slim', 'He's putting on weight' Yeh that's quite different of course, different types of language aren't they? . . . What's the opposite of 'He's quite slim'? . . . well maybe we wouldn't describe people in those terms, we'd just say 'He's quite slim', 'He's quite tall', 'He's not very tall', 'He's quite slim' 'He's got black hair' and then 'fair hair' and then [pause 10 seconds]. OK well let's hope we may develop those a bit in a minute.*

(D7)

For him and those like him, the nature of the linguistic content in a task is of great importance.

Designers falling into the second category clearly regard linguistic content as a secondary issue, and are likely to design tasks where the language to be used is either unspecified, or in some cases only tenuously related to the *describing people* function specified by the brief. For task-oriented designers, the production of an interesting, motivating, meaningful task is paramount. D6 is the best example of this in our data. Soon after reading through the brief, he makes his priorities clear:

> *It* [the task] *has got to be somehow interesting. They* [the learners] *have got to be finding out something new about themselves if it is going to have any impact on their minds.*
>
> (D6)

His design strategy is very breadth first, and during the course of his *Explore* he looks at no fewer that five genres/scenarios before selecting which one to develop. Two of his main concerns with all these genres/scenarios are firstly their <u>affective content</u> – whether they will threaten learners or put them at ease – and secondly whether they will help them to develop as individuals. At no point in this *Explore* does he consider language content in any detail. In fact language content does not concern him until very late in his design, at the point where he is writing the TN for his main activity. Even then the reference is very insubstantial, considerably shorter than those of D15 that we considered on p. 103. Here it is in its entirety:

> *I will give them an e.g. here: e.g. 'Would person "X" make a good waitress, lawyer, midwife?' No that's a bit loaded* [midwife], *'waitress, lawyer'.*
>
> (D6)

Language or task orientations are particularly manifested in starting points. The language-oriented designers have as a strategy (which, as we saw in the last chapter, they do not always follow!) to identify real-life *describing people* situations and their language output. They then sift through these to find one suitable for pedagogic exploitation. The task-oriented designer starts by looking for activities that possess certain characteristics and then seeks ways of fitting *describing people* language into one of these. In the case of D6, these characteristics relate to interest and impact. For D2, another task-oriented designer,[6] the characteristic relates to a particular genre. Immediately after his *Read brief* he says:

> *Well, my thought there when I was reading it is that clearly some kind of task which involves the differential distribution of information as in a*

jigsaw activity. Now that could be that different members of the class are given actual information or that they are given a framework within which they provide their own information and that they have an outcome which can only be reached by obtaining that information from each other so some kind of survey activity is one fairly obvious way of doing it. I tend to think of this as some kind of matrix in which there is categories of information along one dimension and identities of names of individuals down in the other dimension.

(D2)

He then puts his energies into finding a way of inserting the *describing people* function into this framework.

It is natural to ask which of these orientations is the more successful. Opinions about the role of language content in teaching methodology are doubtless deep-seated in language teachers' views of the pedagogic world, and one might imagine that any attempt at task evaluation is likely simply to reflect the evaluators' perspective on this issue. As it happens, the teacher evaluations to be reported in Chapter 8 rate D2 (a task-oriented designer) very highly, while the task of D7 (a language-oriented designer) is placed by some evaluators in the 'five least preferred tasks' category. But, as we shall discuss in Chapter 8, it is not in fact the case that these evaluators show a strong task-oriented bias. Language content is certainly not a criterion they ignore.

6.2.7 Timing

In order to discover whether any differences of emphasis occur between the S and NS/T groups as they map out their tasks, a count was made, for both groups, of all the referents coded during *Instantiate*, *Write TN* and *Write WS*. These were then rank ordered to establish (in the crude terms that a numerical count can provide) their comparative importance for each group. This exercise revealed very few differences, suggesting that during the processes of instantiation and TN/WS writing designers from both groups are dealing substantially with the same issues. Perhaps the most prominent difference relates to timing.

The timing factor proves a problem for many designers, who are being asked not just to produce a task for class use, but for a specific slot of no more than 30 minutes. Though there are one or two designers who cavalierly refuse to be affected by such mundane factors, most take the time constraint seriously. Indeed many, from both groups, end up having to modify their tasks to make them fit in with the time available. Overall, there are more occurrences of the <u>timing</u> code among

S than NS/T designers. But the NS/T group tend to bring up the issue earlier in the design process, and for some it is clearly a question of central importance. Here are D10's comments just after she has finished reviewing the brief:

> *OK let me just review the main things again. So it's adults, monolingual, intermediate level 15 to 20 in the class, descriptions of character and physical appearance and it's for speaking and you've got 30 minutes maximum so that could be less. Now the activity if it is going to be no more than half an hour it's going to be important to have a feedback stage at the end so that might take at least 10 minutes of the time. 10 minutes feedback so that leaves 20 minutes for the rest of the class.*

(D10)

In the case of this particular designer, timing becomes something of an obsession. It dominates her design throughout, and when she reviews her task at the end of the session, she concentrates wholly on the timing issue, descending into astonishing detail. Should the learners be allowed two or three minutes silent thinking time? Is eight minutes enough for a final feedback session, or should ten be allowed? Is five or seven minutes allowable for learner talking time? These are perhaps the questions of a teacher writing the plan for a lesson she will herself teach.

Sections 6.2.6 and 6.2.7 have been concerned with differences between designers. They suggest that:

- designers tend to be either language- or task-oriented. The former show great concern for the language content of tasks. The latter are more concerned with developing meaningful and interesting activities. There is no obvious association between one of these orientations and successful task design;
- timing is an important issue for many designers. NS/T designers tend to bring up the issue earlier, and for some it becomes a central variable in the design process.

6.2.8   Writing the TN and WS

Points made throughout the second half of this chapter relate to the *Write TN* and *Write WS* macrostages as well as *Instantiate*, and there is little specific to the former two that needs adding. The quotation below from D8 shows how many designers write their TN and WS. He appears to begin with a statement of the value of *Write WS* in revising tasks ('appears' only because part of his sentence is indistinct). The quotation well exemplifies the process of instantiation continuing, with the task being elaborated and modified as the WS gets written. The example also illustrates a species of the *review* → *modify* cycle discussed earlier. D8's procedure is to state a sentence, read it through (a type of review) then add a detail or modify it. The details of this quotation are difficult to follow, but these points stand clear:

> *Right so I might as well start with the worksheets because that may show how if there are some problems hidden in the [unclear]. Better to [unclear] before we spend too much time writing out the, revising the cards. So better call this something – Guess Who? OK that'll do for now – [writing] Guess Who? And [writing] Instructions. In groups of, groups of what? 3 or 4, your task is to ask and answer questions about a famous character, about a famous person. In groups of 3 or 4 your task is to ask and answer questions about a famous person, ask and answer questions about a famous person, is to ask and answer questions in order to find out who is on the card – this is the intermediate level – groups of 3 or 4 your task is to ask and answer questions about a famous person, groups of 3 or 4 your task is to ask and answer questions, is to try to find out, in groups of 3 or 4 your task is to guess who, task is to play a game to find out who the person is, who the people are, who the people are on the cards. In groups of 3 or 4 your task is to play a game to find out who the people are on the card, on the what cards?, on the cards, on the cards provided, you are provided with, the teacher will give you, on the cards. In groups of 3 or 4 your task is to play a game to find out who the people are on the cards.*

(D8)

A number of S designers <u>philosophise</u> on the role and nature of TNs, and some of their views are included in Appendix 5.

6.2.9   Important issues raised in section 6.2

One of the major themes of this section has been how designers manage to achieve the degree of attention to detail necessary for successful task design and how, once this has been achieved, they manage to control it such that the design does not become bogged down. Writing TN and WS are, we have seen, naturally activities in which a great deal of detail has to be handled, and by extending instantiation into these macrostages the designer is able to ensure that details play a role in the design process. We have also seen that cyclic designing can manage an

Designing Language Teaching Tasks: Middles and Ends 125

'even descent into detail'. Processes like reviewing and other metacognitive devices (e.g. state of play statements) help to prevent designers from losing themselves in the welter of detail which occur during cyclic design. A main function of these devices is to ensure that the changing state of an emerging task is monitored as developments and modifications are adopted. 'Concrete visualisation capacity', supported by the simulation process, helps to provide rapid development and evaluation of task possibilities as they occur, so that quick decisions can be made regarding proposals that have been at least partially developed.

The section has also continued with the theme of comparative enrichment in S designers' work. The major characteristic discussed here in relation to this has been 'maximum variable control'. S designers simply attend to and take on board more factors than their NS/T counterparts.

7
The Good Task Designer: Some Hypotheses

7.1 A general characterisation

The study that has been reported in this book has to be regarded as a preliminary one. The data we have considered have been restricted, and although we have covered them in some detail, the assumption has always been that the study's main purpose is to suggest hypotheses which will need small-scale controlled research to verify.

In this chapter we shall review the preliminary findings reported in earlier ones, and restate them in summary form as a set of hypotheses regarding what characteristics the good task designer (the GTD hereafter) might possess. But we shall begin by attempting to relate our emerging portrait of the GTD to the view of expertise described in Chapter 2 in relation to the work of Bereiter & Scardamalia (1993).

The characterisation of expertise which Bereiter & Scardamalia provide is based on something of a paradox. Accumulated research into expertise places emphasis on the expert's possession of elaborate and rich domain knowledge. In this view, the expert is saved the effort of highly demanding computations and thought processes precisely by the possession of this domain knowledge. It is the novice who has to work hard because he does not have a repertoire to fall back on. So in the realm of chess playing for example, the novice has to work through chess positions as if for the first time, while the expert, who has come across similar positions before, brings with him strategies for handling them, held in repertoire, which can be reapplied. The same holds for medical diagnosis. The novice has to think the new case through, while the expert has seen so many similar ones that the same degree of effort is not required.

The paradox comes about because this characterisation of the expert suggests that it is he, rather than the novice, who will satisfice. The expert (this characterisation suggests) just plucks ideas from repertoire with the minimum of effort, solving the problem in half the time and with half the effort of the novice, who has to strain to the limit to achieve the same. But this is just not what happens – at least not in the case of writing, the area of expertise which Bereiter & Scardamalia have studied particularly closely. Expert writers do not satisfice. It is they who agonise, not the novices. To repeat a quotation we gave in Chapter 2: 'many experts we know', Bereiter & Scardamalia (1993: 34) say, 'are active striving people. They work long hours…and they tend to set standards for themselves and others that are always at least slightly beyond reach.' They put a great deal of effort into their work, even though they do not, strictly speaking, have to.

Bereiter & Scardamalia's characterisation of expertise contains a further element. They argue that experts (unlike novices) are able not just to utilise domain knowledge when undertaking some specific task requiring expertise. But they can also transfer into their domain knowledge what they learn by doing the specific task. What they know beforehand helps what they do, but what they do becomes part of what they know also. The traffic is two-way.

What we have found in this study fits in well with Bereiter & Scardamalia's view of expertise. Paralleling the arguments just made, we might have expected to find the novice designing effortfully from scratch, in contrast to the expert who has plenty of material in repertoire that can be drawn upon. This 'material' may include entire tasks dealing with the relevant language area (*describing people* in our case). But it will go far beyond that, to encompass sets of techniques for setting up group-work, for revising language content, for preparing learners for a class activity, for writing TNs. Indeed the expert's domain knowledge will cover practically all aspects of the design activity being asked of him. One might expect the expert task designer to satisfice. But the S designers do not satisfice that much. Their designs are richer, more complex than those of the NS/Ts. They cover more variables, they visualise more concrete detail. And they seem to create or invent issues to complexify far beyond what is necessary.

In addition, there are occasional hints – no more – of two-way traffic in our data. One occurs in the protocol of D6. At a certain point he proposes an exercise where the learners read a selected text and underline parts of it which they think could be used to describe members of the class. D6 considers the possible general use of this exercise type:

How complicated is that exercise? That's a new idea, that is quite a nice idea. I wonder if it's generative for other things. I wonder if I could use that applied to other things ... Maybe that's a new exercise type. Obviously it harps back to the old exercises, reading the text and choosing the sentences you like or dislike, which is powerful even if it's an old chestnut. Here it's not like or dislike, here it's what applies to people in this group. It might actually also allow them to say things about other people in the group which they wouldn't say if they had to construct them and write them down themselves.

(D6)

In these ways, Bereiter & Scardamalia's (1993) model of expertise fits in well with what we have been describing. We turn now to the details of what this study has revealed.

7.2   Characteristics of the good task designer

In this section we shall review the main findings made in Chapters 4–6. We shall do this from the particular perspective of considering what those chapters tell us about good design practice. The findings will be expressed as hypotheses about the characteristics and behaviours of GTDs. We shall therefore in general avoid statements about what less experienced task designers do. So we will not talk about NS/T designers' 'comparative impoverishment', but rather of S designers' 'comparative enrichment'.

The characteristics are reviewed under two main headings. The first is 'logistical control'. This contains all aspects of what we have earlier called 'control', but is somewhat broader and also includes procedures and strategies for the handling of task design. The second heading is 'enrichment' and covers everything to do with how designers ensure that their design is sufficiently detailed and rich. There are, naturally, points at which these two headings overlap, and one can imagine some items appearing under either heading. For example, we noted in Chapter 5 that S designers (like NS/Ts) use repertoire a lot. We have considered this under 'enrichment' because the possession of an elaborate repertoire is indeed part of what enables the S designer to make his design rich. But use of repertoire is also a logistical mechanism that plays an important part in how designers are able to manage the complexities of the design process. A second example is the fact that S designers (again like NS/Ts) carry on their instantiations into the *Write TN/WS* macrostage. This is categorised under 'logistical control'. But because *Write TN/WS* is the macrostage at which a great deal of detail occurs, the strategy may be seen as one that enriches.

The main purpose of this section is indeed to identify characteristics and behaviours that facilitate good design. But we also include statements about what good designers may *not* do, and identify points that may *not* be important. For example, we make mention of the fact that S designers may have either a language or a task orientation. The implication is that either orientation may lead to successful design.

The characteristics covered are looked at only briefly, because we are here concerned with review. For each, we provide a short explanatory statement and where possible an example or a reference back to an earlier chapter. The headings appear as firm statements because it would be tedious to include hedges throughout. But these hedges should be understood. For example, the first characteristic considered below is stated thus: 'GTDs have "concrete visualisation capacity".' This is to be understood as 'The hypothesis is that GTDs may have "concrete visualisation capacity".'

7.2.1 Logistical control

GTDs have 'concrete visualisation capacity'

This is the ability to envisage possibilities (candidate classroom activities for example) in some degree of concrete detail. In Chapter 4 we noted that D1 showed evidence of it, but it has been mainly covered in Chapter 6, where we considered it under two headings, (a) and (b) below.

(a) GTDs simulate input and output a lot

Simulating is defined in Appendix 1 as 'verbalising what it is imagined that a learner or teacher would say or think'. Simulating output is the code used when a designer verbalises expected learner words or thoughts, while simulate input refers to what the teacher may say or think. Simulation is an important tool enabling designers to descend into detail, as design proceeds. It also helps designers to identify issues that might otherwise not come to light.

Chapter 6 describes D8 beginning his instantiation by rehearsing what the learners might say during the task he is developing. This simulate output leads him to identify one problem and to make one decision. That chapter also includes an example of D10 simulating input. In her case it was thought that working out in advance what she will say to the learners was providing her with a degree of security.

(b)   GTDs explore possibilities rapidly but with some degree of detail

The second aspect of concrete visualisation capacity is that designers often quickly map out possibilities in a highly concrete way. Speed is important to ensure that a number of possibilities may be surveyed and evaluated in a reasonable time. But degree of detail helps to make sensible evaluation feasible. The example of this given in Chapter 6 was of D4 as she considered possible input carriers for her task. She outlined various possibilities in a very short space of time, and was able to consider what each implied in terms of possible activities and classroom configurations.

GTDs have 'easy abandonment capacity'

This is the preparedness to abandon a task or task component after a considerable time has been spent developing it. In a skill like task design where considerations of detail can lead to major modifications, it is important for the designer to show willingness to change direction even at a late stage. This capacity also ensures that a designer does not commit himself to a task simply on the basis of the amount of time that has been spent developing it. In Chapter 6 we saw an example of easy abandonment capacity in the pilot designer who spent an entire hour trying to taskify one real world situation, which she then dropped.

We also noted in the same chapter that importing a task wholesale from repertoire can be motivated by a reluctance to abandon something already worked out. This is a dangerous practice unless the designer is prepared to make changes in the task to make it suit the design brief.

GTDs tend to do one thing at a time

Task design is by its very nature an activity which involves handling a number of variables almost simultaneously, and for this reason designers are inevitably involved in near simultaneous planning on various levels. But there is some small amount of evidence that S designers have a tendency where possible to deal with separate issues one at a time. In Chapter 5 we considered the question brief behaviour of S and NS/T designers and found that the NS/T group tend to ask questions about the brief as they read it, while the S group ask questions afterwards. This led to a tentative suggestion that S designers might be more coherent in their designs.

GTDs spend time analysing the design problem they face

S designers spend more time (an average of 4.65 minutes) at the *Analyse* macrostage than NS/T designers (average 2.67 minutes). Some activities which occur at this macrostage are considered separately below. Taken together they may be considered important to task design, and worthy of attention.

GTDs spend time reviewing what is required of them (as stated in the brief)

All the S designers bar one have a microstage coded as <u>review brief</u>. At this microstage designers go through the brief checking on salient points (and often writing them down). Spending time on <u>review brief</u> helps to ensure that the constraints identified in the brief are fully met by the task designed. D7's <u>review brief</u> action boxes, given on p. 76, illustrate how an S designer goes about reviewing the brief.

GTDs identify procedures and highlight important considerations early on

Identifying design procedures and highlighting important points are further activities undertaken at the *Analyse* macrostage. We associate these activities with Schoenfeld's 'identifying perspectives, frameworks, and important considerations', which he regards as characteristics of good mathematical problem solving.

Chapter 4 contains an example of D1 identifying the procedure he will follow in his design (first to think of a purpose for his task, and then to identify a suitable genre). He does this immediately after he has read through the brief. At the same point in his design, D6 highlights the need for a task that will have interest for, and impact on, his learners. We noted in Chapter 5 that there is considerable variety in the procedures that different designers identify, and in what they highlight.

GTDs practise 'consequence identification'

In discussion of the *Analyse* macrostage we also noted that some designers immediately seek the consequences of issues raised in terms of the intended task. This practice helps to ensure that discussion of issues is purposeful and consequential. Chapter 5 contains several examples of this. In one, D6 considers what the lack of information about learner nationality will imply for the tasks he is designing.

GTDs tend to make higher-level decisions before lower-level ones

In Chapter 5 we distinguish three code levels. Level 1 codes, like <u>type</u> and <u>genre</u>, are relatively abstract. Level 3 codes deal with concrete, 'mechanical' aspects of tasks, such as <u>configuration,</u> <u>props</u> and <u>stage</u>. At the intermediate Level 2 comes <u>scenario</u> – a task scenario may be seen as a concrete realisation of a type or genre. S designers tend to make higher-level decisions before lower-level ones. This is shown in Figure 5.5.

A significant number of NS/T designers seem to move to the design of parts when the shape of the whole has not been fully conceived. An example is D15, who after reviewing the brief, moves almost immediately into planning of the first stage of his task.

GTDs do not always do what they say they will do

A substantial number of designers suggest (rather explicitly) that the process of task design should begin with the identification of real world situations in which the language points to be taught would naturally be used. One of these is then 'taskified'. But designers do not in general do this. There may be reasons for this associated with the particular function (*describing people*) dealt with in this study, but it is perhaps that designers generally are flexible in the way they approach design, whatever algorithm exists in their head. Some designer statements that they will taskify a real world situation are given on p. 90.

GTDs sometimes design in an opportunistic way

This is related to the point above. In opportunistic design a matter is dealt with almost incidentally when it comes up in a context where some other issue is being considered. An example given (in Chapter 5) was how D2 decided on a groupwork configuration. He is in fact considering possible information gap scenarios. The groupwork decision emerges from his consideration of one particular scenario, which he goes on to reject.

GTDs use a breadth-first (BF) strategy

A BF strategy is one in which the designer considers a number of possibilities (for a task or task component) in brief before selecting one for further development. The advantage of this strategy is that it avoids too early a commitment to one solution which may, after lengthy development, turn out to be unsuitable. The concomitant disadvantage is that it is heavy on channel capacity, since the designer has to hold various possibilities in memory before selecting one. The alternative to BF is depth-first (DF), where one solution is explored to the full from the start.

When it comes to selection of a task (scenario, type or genre) for development, S designers tend to be BF. This is evidenced by the fact (reviewed later in this chapter) that they spend time on the *Explore* macrostage. One of the examples given in Chapter 6 was D6. During his *Explore* he looks at five possible genres and scenarios, spending an average of 6 minutes on each (i.e. a good 30 minutes overall) before selecting one for further development.

GTDs display metacognition

Schoenfeld (1985) uses the term 'control' to describe what is more generally known as 'metacognition' – strategies used to monitor, assess and manage behaviour. Metacognition has been discussed in relation to many skills, and is generally thought to be associated with expertise. In Chapter 6 we looked at various aspects of designers' metacognitive strategies. One of these relates to evaluative behaviour, associated with the evaluate code, and marked also by codes like alternative and reject. In the case of all these codes, we find more occurrences in S than NS/T designer protocols. A lengthy example of evaluation was given from D1's protocol at the point where he is considering various possible describees. In the case of almost all of the many alternatives he considers, there is an evaluate, followed by a reject, a fix, or a maintain.

Another code associated with metacognition is state of play. This reports metacomments by designers on the point in the design process they are at, and may be statements of what has been done, what they are doing, or what is to be done, possibly next. S designers use state of play a lot, often following an evaluation or some development of a task. We note in Chapter 6 that the sequence *propose alternative → evaluate → state of play → 'move on'* is a common one. One example given of the use of state of play showed summary action boxes of D8 writing his TN and WS. His use of this code is associated with transitions between microstages; whenever something is decided or changed, it is signalled by a state of play.

GTDs Instantiate while they Write TN/WS

Some may be tempted to propose a task design model in which the writing of TN or WS takes place at a final stage, and simply involves committing to paper decisions already made at the *Instantiate* macrostage. Although some designers do this, many use the *Write TN/WS* macrostages either to continue instantiating or even to undertake the major part of instantiation. Although the *create → write down* model has a certain logic and elegance, it is almost inevitable that some detailed design should occur at the *Write TN/WS* macrostages. Also, as we noted earlier in this chapter, task design is a skill in which considerations of detail can lead to major modifications. So there are occasionally advantages to allowing details emerging during *Write TN/WS* to have their effect on a task's overall shape. An example of details being added to a task during *Write TN/WS* is given in Chapter 4, where D1 adds 'burglar' to the describee list (thus injecting a touch of humour into the task). He also adds a final follow-up stage which has not been previously discussed.

At times, GDTs design cyclically

Adding to a task at the *Write TN/WS* macrostages is an example of cyclic design, a phenomenon which occurs more generally. This is the process whereby a designer returns on a number of occasions to his emerging task, on each occasion adding more detail. In Chapter 6 we noted a common strategy involving cyclic design. In this, the designer creates the outline of a task. He then reviews this outline, and during the course of this review, or after it, adds some new detail. Because the new detail has led to a revised (and more detailed) framework, this sparks off a fresh review which in turn leads to a new detail. One of the examples of cyclic design given in Chapter 6 came from D11's *Instantiate.* We plotted the development of her task through a number of 'passes', as it changed from an idea for a genre into a fully fledged scenario, with details worked out.

GTDs descend into detail evenly

A main advantage of cyclic design is that it allows details to be added to a task in a gradual fashion, such that it is possible for the designer to monitor developments as they occur. This is associated with what we called an 'even descent into detail'. The design process involves handling a large number of variables almost simultaneously, and if a single variable is highly developed at an early stage, the result is likely to be that the variable will control the task's development, possibly to an undesirable extent. An example of overdevelopment of one variable is D10's near obsession with timing, which drives most of her design process.

GTDs maintain tally of task modifications and developments by constant reviewing

Another major way in which designers keep control over the addition of details to a task is by constant reviewing. The rule seems to be, we noted, that *if anything changes, go back through what has been decided to establish how things now stand.* On p. 113 we noted the number of <u>reviews</u> which occurred in D11's *Instantiate* as she went through the various passes in the development of her task. Like <u>state of play</u> (and <u>identify issue</u>), the <u>review</u> code operates as a 'change instigator code'. Its use often signals transition to a new topic.

GTDs can be either language- or task-oriented

In Chapter 6 we noted that although all our subjects share a common 'communicative' perspective, differences in designing style are apparent. The major one relates to whether a designer is language- or task-oriented.

A language-oriented designer shows a great deal of concern for the language content of his task, viewing the task as a vehicle for language practice. The task-oriented designer, on the other hand, has as his main concern to develop a task that will be interesting and meaningful for the learners. For him, language content is a secondary issue.

Our example of a language-oriented designer was D7, and Chapter 6 contains a list of some of his concerns relating to language content. This orientation is reflected in the starting point for design, and D7 was one of those who expressed the intention to begin by considering real world situations and the language used in them. D6 was given as the example of a task-oriented designer. His identified procedure at the outset is to find a task which will hold interest and impact. He spends almost no time at all on establishing language content.

GTDs show much individual variation

Chapter 5 contains another example of designer differences. In Figure 5.3, the points highlighted by designers early in the designer procedure are listed, and the list shows considerable variation. We point out there that such differences become important if one is attempting to train individuals in task design. Training programmes must allow flexibility in various directions, and avoid prescribing algorithms in areas where individual design styles operate.

7.2.2 Enrichment

GTDs have 'task logistics sensitivity'

This was defined in Chapter 4 as 'the characteristic of showing awareness of problems and issues related to the mechanics of setting up and conducting class activities'. It was mentioned in relation to D1. The example given from his protocol was the issue he raises in relation to a 'guess who is being described' game. He notes that unless care is taken, it will be possible to identify the describee very quickly. For example, if a person is described as wearing glasses, that may narrow down the field to just one or two; so the activity may not take very long. This characteristic is not taken up in later chapters, and can therefore only be said to have been partially explored.

GTDs show 'learner/context sensitivity'

'Learner/context sensitivity' is awareness of the learners and their context. One dimension of it is related to learner characteristics associated with culture. A number of designers, for example, are aware that in some cultures a learner talking in front of the class might be viewed as 'showing off', while in other cultures it may simply be viewed as natural and co-operative behaviour. Designers know that the former attitude can pose major problems for certain sorts of language teaching speaking activities, and this knowledge may affect their choice of task.

NS/T designers question the brief more than S designers regarding learner/context attributes, and seem ill at ease with the lack of contextual detail the design brief provides. But when it comes to actual designing, it is S designers who pay more attention to these factors. To suggest this, in Chapter 5 we identified a family of codes showing 'learning/contextual orientation' and noted the high occurrence of this code family in S designer protocols.

GTDs spend time exploring

S designers spend time exploring possible task types/genres/scenarios (the *Explore* macrostage). This fact is highly associated with the BF strategy that S designers use. As well as being a useful strategy to adopt for design (preventing too early commitment to any one task, as discussed earlier in this chapter), having lengthy *Explore* macrostages also provides a degree of choice from which the designer can select. It contributes, in other words, to the enrichment of the design. We have already seen an example of an *Explore* earlier in this chapter (that of D6). A further example is given in Figure 6.1. It illustrates how one designer considers the possible taskification of six real world situations, before choosing one to develop in her *Instantiate*.

GTDs use repertoire a lot

Both S and NS/T designers take ideas for actual tasks from repertoire, and if one widens the net to consider activities and procedures within tasks then the role repertoire plays is substantial. Repertoire use can in theory lead to satisficing, where an element is unthinkingly adopted from some other source. But with proper use a large repertoire provides a rich resource from which items may be taken. D7 is an example of a designer who admits taking his task from repertoire. As his consideration of language content (exemplified earlier in this chapter) shows, this does not prevent him from putting full energy into meeting the specific requirements set out in the design brief.

GTDs create choices

A major reason for the enrichment of S designer protocols is that they seem wherever possible to create choices. This is signalled not just by the existence of *Explore* macrostages, but also by the occurrence of codes such as <u>alternative</u> and <u>reject</u>. Various illustrations of choice creation are given in Chapter 6. One involves D4 considering possible input carriers for her task. She signals that she is consciously considering various possibilities (she is *just running through possibilities here*), and looks at spoken, written and visual candidates – email, tape recording, photo and video.

GTDs indulge in 'self-imposed complexification'

Closely associated with choice creation is what we call 'self-imposed complexification'. This is where the designer appears deliberately to make the design task more complex than it needs to be, by introducing issues that it would not be necessary to consider just to design the task with minimum effort. An example of self-imposed complexification is given from the protocol of D7 and the way he introduces issues regarding language content that are not strictly necessary for the task to be developed.

GTDs show maximum variable control

When S designers produce tasks they do so with attention given to a wide range of variables so that their tasks are sensitive to as many issues and constraints as possible. One of the examples given in Chapter 6 relates to how gender is handled by D5. He (as well as D8) takes pains to produce a task which will be appropriate for and interesting to female as well as male learners.

7.3 Are the experts expert? By nature or nurture?

Any statements about GTDs need to be based on a conviction that those task designers who have been studied are indeed 'good'. Is this true of our S designers? They are, basically, individuals who have had a lot of experience at task design, and for the most part have become famous by writing EFL textbooks. But experience does not necessarily lead to expertise, nor alas does fame necessarily reflect any expertise other than how to become published by the right publishers! In the following, final, chapter, we consider an attempt to evaluate the tasks of our S designers by some more objective criterion than the good names of their creators. We also raise the issue, very briefly, of task design training – can good task design be taught?

8
Evaluating and Teaching Task Design

8.1 How expert are the experts?

In Chapter 2 we noted that traditional expert–novice studies select their experts using 'external' or 'social' criteria; an expert is someone who is recognised as one within society. One of the criteria society is likely to put much store by is length of experience. As we saw in that chapter, there are problems with this notion of expertise, and in this context we noted the old adage that one teacher may have had ten years of experience, while another may have had one year's experience ten times. This is the phenomenon that led Bereiter & Scardamalia (1993) to distinguish between an *expert* and an *experienced non-expert*.

The criteria that we used to identify our S designer group were 'external' and 'social'. To be a member of this group an individual had to have spent at least five years engaged in a major way in task design. All S designers are in fact well-known individuals with established reputations in the materials design and language teaching methodology areas. Given these criteria, the question arises how we know that they are experts as opposed to experienced non-experts.

Again as we noted in Chapter 2, some in the literature (in Ericsson & Smith 1991b for example) argue that we require a performance-related measure of expertise. We need to evaluate performance at some activity which is felt to encapsulate expertise in a particular domain. The task design brief given to our subjects is our attempt to create such an activity. But what we have so far not considered is how well our subjects, S and NS/T designers alike, perform that activity as measured in some independent way. We have, in other words, taken it for granted that S designer tasks are 'better' than those produced by the NS/T group. But are they?

In this section we shall consider some pilot work undertaken to provide external evaluation of our designers' tasks, in order to establish whether the S group are indeed experts not just by reputation but also by performance. It is perhaps worth reiterating a point made in Chapter 2, that despite discussion in the literature of the need for evaluations of performance, it is perfectly common procedure in that literature to use social judgements as well. Thus Bereiter & Scardamalia themselves partly identify good writers by their reputations as such, while de Groot's work in chess is based on groupings which take into account social recognition (as 'grand masters', etc.). Although it is proper to desire evaluation of performance, expertise studies do also rely on 'social' criteria.

The work described in this section was for the most part undertaken by Virginia Samuda.[1] In order to evaluate the tasks of our 16 designers, she first had to put their tasks in a final format, fit for consumption by external evaluators. Although we had asked designers to complete their tasks in as much detail as possible, only a few (quite understandably given the time constraints) had produced task specifications sufficiently detailed and clear to be comprehensible to outsiders. Fine-tuning the tasks turned out to be a time-consuming and sometimes difficult exercise. Once it was completed, the next stage was to impose a degree of standardisation on the tasks so that they could be compared. Each task was therefore reduced to a set maximum of one side of A4, a limit that had to include the bare essentials of all TN and WS material. The final versions of all tasks appear in Appendix 6.

Ten experienced teachers of EFL undertook the task evaluations for us. Five of these were students on the M.Ed. in TESOL programme at the University of Leeds School of Education. The remaining five were doctoral students at the same institution, and were all teachers with EFL experience and research interests. Nine of the evaluators were non-native speakers of English. Three were from Iran, two from Japan, and one each from Argentina, Hong Kong, Macedonia, Saudi Arabia and the UK.

For the purposes we are concerned with here, it was felt sufficient to elicit only the most general comments on our tasks.[2] The evaluators were therefore simply asked to select the five activities they <u>most preferred</u> and the five they <u>least preferred</u> from the collection, and to put their choices in rank order. They were also asked to give the reasons for their selections, saying for each task what they particularly liked or disliked. The only other guidance given was that evaluation should be made in relation to the design brief, and not in terms of any other criteria, such as how well the activities might suit their own particular students.

Figure 8.1 shows the number of nominations each task received (from all evaluators) for the most preferred and least preferred categories. As these figures show, it is not the case that absolutely all the S designer tasks are favoured over absolutely all the NS/T tasks, nor the NS/T tasks disfavoured over all the S tasks. But in the most preferred category, there is a distinct grouping of S tasks at the top of the list and NS/T tasks at the bottom, while in the least preferred category this is reversed. Figure 8.2 shows the percentages of overall nominations for most/least preferred categories in terms of our two groups, S and NS/T designers. The figure indicates that 69 per cent of the nominations for most preferred task are those of S designers, while 60 per cent of the least preferred category are for NS/T designers.

In order to determine whether the amount by which these percentages are different from 50 per cent is statistically significant, a permutation test was carried out. This had as its null hypothesis that evaluators' choices were completely unrelated to whether the tasks were

Most preferred tasks

Designer	Whether S or NS/T	Number of nominations
D2	S	7
D1	S	6
D4	S	5
D6	S	4
D13	NS/T	4
D3	S	4
D7	S	4
D16	NS/T	3
D15	NS/T	3
D8	S	2
D5	S	2
D11	NS/T	1
D12	NS/T	1
D10	NS/T	1
D17	NS/ I	1
D14	NS/T	1
Total number of nominations[3]		49

Least preferred tasks

Designer	Whether S or NS/T	Number of nominations
D10	NS/T	9
D17	NS/T	8
D12	NS/T	6
D3	S	5
D7	S	4
D6	S	3
D16	NS/T	3
D4	S	3
D5	S	2
D8	S	1
D2	S	1
D11	NS/T	1
D14	NS/T	1
D15	NS/T	1
D1	S	0
D13	NS/T	0
		48

Figure 8.1   Overall ranking: most preferred tasks/least preferred tasks

	Most preferred tasks	Least preferred tasks
S designer tasks	69%	40%
NS/T designer tasks	31%	60%

Figure 8.2 Percentages of total nominations for most/least preferred tasks, in terms of S and NS/T designer groups

designed by S or NS/T designers. For the most preferred tasks the test was significant at the 0.2 per cent level. This can be interpreted as providing very strong evidence that the evaluators are systematically favouring S designer tasks. For the least preferred tasks the result was only significant at the 10 per cent level. This can be interpreted as meaning that there is some, but not strong, evidence that the evaluators are systematically associating NS/T designer tasks with this category. It is important to add that these results are substantially affected by the judgements of one evaluator, identified as 'Evaluator J'. He stands alone in selecting five NS/T tasks as his most preferred choices, and five S tasks as his least preferred. If Evaluator J is removed from consideration, the correlations described above (between S designer tasks and most preferred on the one hand, and NS/T tasks and least preferred on the other) would be extremely statistically significant. But why should this one evaluator have selected in the way he did? Nothing that is known about him as an individual or the context in which he teaches suggests an explanation. Nor does a consideration of the reasons he gives for his choices. The evaluative criteria he uses are the same as those utilised by the other evaluators (to be discussed below), but he uses them quite differently. So while another evaluator finds D12's task 'confusing', Evaluator J praises its 'easy instructions'. Similarly, as Figure 8.1 shows, D17's task is the second least popular overall, and is described by one evaluator as 'boring'. Yet it is one of Evaluator J's favourites, and he finds it 'exciting'. Other examples could be added to show that J is out of step with the other evaluators. But given the rather bare information our evaluative exercise provides, we are unable to say why this should be.[4]

Apart from this general finding, the figures also reveal some interesting details. If we confine discussion to those tasks receiving three or more nominations in each category (most and least preferred), we find five tasks that make an appearance in both camps. These are the tasks of S designers D3, D4, D6 and D7 and of NS/T designer D16. How can this be accounted for? It is possible that some of the tasks were seen as original and out of the ordinary (particularly D6's perhaps), and this might have led some evaluators to put them in the <u>most preferred</u> category. But they also might be regarded by some as idiosyncratic, and hence <u>least preferred</u> for those who do not admire those particular idiosyncrasies. If we look at the actual evaluator comments, good and bad, made in relation to the work of these five designers, we see that in general the evaluators find the same types of characteristics to like in each of them, and other types of characteristics to dislike. So (Evaluator J apart) it is not the case that one evaluator praises a task for one characteristic and another evaluator condemns it for that same characteristic. For example, all the evaluators who place D3's task in the <u>most preferred</u> category do so because they find it 'fun' or 'interesting' – characteristics we associate in Figure 8.3 with the 'affect/cognition related' evaluation category. The evaluators who place the task in their <u>least preferred</u> category do so because they find it complex, and expect logistical difficulties with handling it in class. These are reasons which are associated with Figure 8.3's 'logistics related' category. The 'fun/interesting versus logistically difficult' dimension occurs in relation to a number of these tasks and is certainly a dimension worth further investigation.[5] As a second example, in the case of D4's task three of the five evaluators who place it in the <u>most preferred</u> category actually use the term 'fun' to describe it (other terms used being 'exciting', and 'realistic'). Of the three evaluators who put the same task in the <u>least preferred</u> category, two mention its 'complexity' and the other its 'difficulty'. Differences in overall evaluations thus tend to reflect differing degrees of importance given to different characteristics, rather than disagreements regarding the presence of those characteristics. And these differing degrees of importance will be interesting to study in more depth.

In order to gain some sense of the criteria used by the evaluators, their comments (in relation to <u>most preferred task</u> judgements only) were coded, following where possible the code categories used for protocols. Six general categories were identified, and these appear in Figure 8.3. It is recognised that some of these categories contain a degree of overlap. For example, 'skills related' refers to all comments regarding the skill areas covered in the tasks; evaluators would here be concerned with the coverage given to various of the four skills. This has been kept separate from 'language related', a category which is concerned with the actual exponents, lexis and grammar covered in the task. Despite the separation of these two category types, clearly an argument could be made for considering them together. The figures in the rightmost column refer to the total number of mentions in each category for all the five selected

Evaluation category	Examples of areas commented on	Numbers
Logistics related	Well-organised, manageable, requiring few props	31
Affect/cognition related	Fun, interesting, cognitively challenging, motivating	24
Language related	Good language content, authentic language use	17
Relationship to real world	Realistic activity	9
Skills related	Practises interaction, involves writing as well	8
Learner related	Learner centred, suits learner level	8

Figure 8.3 Criteria used by evaluators (evaluation categories) in relation to their five <u>most preferred</u> tasks, and total number of comments

tasks of all the evaluators. The figure reveals that logistical considerations and 'affect/cognitive related' are the two most popular categories. Language-related points are not ignored however, and this suggests that language-oriented designers do not fare badly in these evaluations because the criteria used are biased against them, a possibiity that was aired in Chapter 6.

It will be clear from the above discussion that this task evaluation exercise had restricted aims. It does not offer anything like a full picture of how tasks are evaluated by teachers. Nor does it consider *learner* reactions to the tasks after their use – a major dimension which a full evaluation would require. Nonetheless the exercise does provide a degree of confirmation that S designers' work is better regarded than that of NS/T designers – by one group of teacher evaluators at least.

8.2 Teaching task design

Schoenfeld (1985) describes a number of studies intended to provide empirical support for his model, and these involve attempts to teach the strategies of mathematical problem solving that he identifies. One of these experiments is based on card sorting – a research technique briefly mentioned in Chapter 1 in which subjects are asked to group together cards which bear examples of the phenomenon the researcher is interested in. A finding in the literature (Chi *et al.* 1981) is that when experts are asked to card sort, they do so according to 'deep structures', using underlying similarities and differences to group items together. Novices on the other hand use 'surface structures', putting together items that share some superficial characteristic. In the experiment Schoenfeld describes, three groups are investigated: experts, novices, and a group of novices who have been given some overt instruction in mathematical problem solving. The result is that the experts and novices do indeed sort using deep and superficial characteristics respectively, thus supporting what is found elsewhere in the literature. Interestingly enough, Schoenfeld's 'instructed novices' fall in the middle – deep similarities are noticed, but not with the sophistication of the expert group. This finding, and others Schoenfeld reports, suggest that there may be benefit to teaching problem-solving skills.

Such a conclusion needs to be tempered, though, by the results of Ericsson & Harris's (1989) study, mentioned on p. 13. They found that chess novices can be taught configurations of moves, but do not thereby become chess masters. It is possible that novices will learn to recognise deep similarities and differences between items, but not thereby become experts. Similar doubts may be raised in relation to the area of language learning strategies. There have been various attempts at 'learner training' in the applied linguistics literature. One pioneering text is Ellis & Sinclair (1989), who in effect offer a self-training manual for language learners. Oxford's (1990) book might also be described as a training manual, and includes exercises geared to develop learning strategies in students. But as to how effective such attempts can be, the jury is still out. As McDonough (1998: 195) puts it, there is not yet 'much hard evidence that strategy training leads to improvement in language learning outcomes'. We do not yet know whether strategies can be taught. One might add to the uncertainty by noting how difficult it would be to judge the success of instruction in this area. The research paradigm which immediately springs to mind would follow a period of strategy teaching with a test to see whether, in comparison with a control group, superior learning had taken place. But the paradigm is fraught with problems. If success is discernible, have we exerted sufficient control over the multifarious variables involved to know which has caused it? And are we able to distinguish a short-term effect from real long-term gain, measured in terms of performance on the whole behaviour itself, and not just in the particular sub-area covered in teaching?

These reservations about whether we can teach and then assess instructional success must be made in relation to task design expertise also. The identification of characteristics associated with good task design can only be part of our efforts to explore how the behaviour can be taught. But, one might argue, it is an important part. Articulation of the hypotheses given in Chapter 7, and indeed this study in general, can be regarded as a step towards the training of task designers. Much more research needs to be done on the training issue, but it is to be hoped that this study provides a start and will be found useful by those involved in training task designers.[6]

8.3 Envoy

Whether or not this study does indeed provide such a start, it has aimed above all to contribute modestly to an area of study little touched on in the applied linguistics literature. This is the study of expertise, not just of task designers, but of all professionals in the language-teaching arena – syllabus designers, teacher educators and even teachers themselves. It is a huge area. As we noted in Chapter 1: 'an entire manifesto of expertise research suggests itself'.

Appendix 1: TADECS Codes with Working Definitions and Notes

D = designer; L = learner; T = teacher. A few entirely self-evident items are not glossed. Some codes have subcategories, which are indented.

CODES	WORKING DEFINITIONS/NOTES
1. STAGES	**Levels of analysis identified in the design process**
1.1 Macrostages	**This list is complete**
Read brief	D reads brief from beginning to end, usually aloud
Analyse	D reviews brief and highlights issues, before beginning design
Explore	D considers various possible options for tasks, before finally deciding on one
Instantiate	Having decided on a final task, D undertakes detailed design
Write WS	Worksheets and other materials to be given to the Ls are produced
Write TN	Production of teachers' notes, or of instructions to be given to another T

1.2 Microstages	**This list is not complete, and only offers examples. Microstages are stated only in terms of codes (operators and referents) occurring in this appendix**
Review brief	D goes over the brief, making sure all required elements are understood and noted
Develop scenario	Having identified a possible task scenario, D now develops it

2. OPERATORS	Cognitive activities Ds engage in
Assume	Make an assumption (e.g. about language knowledge)

Check	Seeking to confirm some piece of information. Check brief is different from Review brief, the latter being a longer and more systematic procedure
Comment	Pass comment on (e.g. a point made in the brief)
Compare	Compare (e.g. two versions of a task)
Consider	Draw attention to and reflect on for a period of time, without the result necessarily being a proposal or systematic development
Describe	E.g. an activity in the teachers' notes
Develop	Expand something already proposed
Draw	A picture, e.g. on blackboard
Evaluate	Conscious attempt to reach a judgement on (e.g.) a task proposal
positive	
negative	
Exemplify	
Explain	
Fix	Reach a decision to adopt something
Highlight	Identify as important
Identify	Identify scenario = simply to acknowledge its existence. Propose scenario = to consider it positively as a possibility for design
Maintain	Leave unchanged, after a process of reconsideration
Manage	Various behaviours associated with control of the design procedure
Modify	Change something already decided on
Note	Write down (e.g.) what has been decided
Propose	Suggest as possible solution/task, etc.
Question	Usually in question brief
Reconsider	
Reject	Decide against (e.g. a proposed scenario)
Review	Going over something (e.g. what has been done; design brief, etc.)

Appendix 1   (*Continued*)

OPERATORS	Cognitive activities Ds engage in
Shelve	Postpone making a decision – a conscious act to put aside (rather than simply the failure to resolve an issue)
Simulate	D's procedure of verbalising what it is imagined an L or T would say or think
Solve	Reach a solution. As in <u>solve issue</u>
Stuck	D does not know what to do next
Philosophise	Talk in a generalised way; draw morals on an issue
Write	

3. REFERENTS	A noun phrase, usually standing as the object of a verb – the operator (though referents in fact encompass a wide variety of semantic relations – see p. 53).
3.1 Artefacts	**Product provided to Ds or produced by them**
Brief	The piece of paper given to Ds describing the task to be designed (given on p. 29)
Task	The overall task designed, with all its stages
Final task	The task which in the event becomes the adopted one
TN	Teachers' notes. This also includes teacher instructions
WS	Worksheet – any and all materials given to the Ls
Notes	These are notes D makes as he goes along. Distinguished from TN or WS

3.2 Design brief related	**Codes related to points mentioned in (or raised in relation to) the design brief given to Ds**
3.2.1 Learner and context-related	
Age	The Ls' age (specified as adult)
Financial status	Whether Ls are rich or poor (unspecified)

Language knowledge	Language that Ls are known to possess already
L identity	Related to L identity in general, not specifically one aspect (e.g. nationality or age)
Level	The Ls' level (specified as intermediate)
Nationality	Nationality of Ls
Previous practice	Practice in the function of describing people (or some other relevant linguistic items) which Ls have already had
Social class	Ls' social class (unspecified)
Study length	How long Ls have been studying English (unspecified)
Class hours	Number of hours Ls are taught per week (specified as 2)
Class size	Number of Ls in class (specified as 15–20)
Course type	Whether general English or some form of ESP (specified as general)
Coursebook	Whether a coursebook is being used (and if so which?)
Gender proportion	Number of males/females in class (unspecified)
Institution type	Type of school Ls are attending (e.g. private or state – unspecified)
Location	Country in which Ls are studying (specified as 'their own country')
Monolingual	Fact that Ls all have the same L1
Teacher	Whether T knows class well
Togetherness	Whether Ls have been together long as a class (and are hence comfortable with each other)

3.2.2 Task related	
Target function	Describing people
Target language	Language items to practise
Skill area	Specified as 'speaking' in the brief
Time available	Time available for task to be done in class (15–30 minutes)
Activity type	Specified as 'communicative' in the brief

Appendix 1   (*Continued*)

Task related	
Interactivity	Fact that Ls are required to interact verbally
Practice exercise	Fact that what is required does not involve presentation of new language

3.2.3 Design related	
Activity unreality	That the target function is not common in real life, particularly in non-monologue form
Design time available	How long D has available to produce a task
Detailed design	Fact that detailed design, with TN and WS, is required
Familiar	Whether or not the D is familiar with some aspect of what is being required
Next day use	The fact that the task must be used the next day
Recipient	D's choice to prepare task for a colleague to teach or for published materials
Brief clarity	Extent to which what the brief requires is clear

3.3 *Attributes*	Terms relevant to the description of tasks or learners
3.3.1 Of tasks	
Authenticity	All discussion of the extent to which a task or the language it elicits are natural in terms of real world behaviour
Affective content	The ways in which a task engages aspects of an L's affect. For example, a task may (undesirably) involve an L in boasting
Cognitive/linguistic challenge	How easy or challenging, in cognitive or linguistic terms, a task is
Communicativity	Extent to which a task is 'communicative'
Material quantity	How many props, WSs, etc. the task requires. Some Ds regard the involvement of minimal materials as a virtue
Atmosphere	The atmosphere (friendly, uncompetitive or otherwise) a task creates in class

Interest level	Whether a task is boring, repetitive or interesting, fun
Logistical challenge	How easy or complex a task is in logistical terms
Meaningfulness	Whether or not a task will be regarded as meaningful by the Ls. This includes discussion of the 'purposefulness' of activities
Novelty	Extent to which a task will be new to Ls (or indeed to the language teaching field as a whole)
Participation level	Issues related to the amount of time participants are engaged in the task, and in ensuring maximum talk time for all participants
Participation orientation	Extent to which task is T or L oriented. This includes issues related to allowing L freedom, developing L self-awareness
Preparedness	Whether or not the task has been sufficiently prepared by the designer

3.3.2 Of learners	
Communicative willingness	Extent to which Ls will be prepared to communicate orally with each other
L interests	L interests
Touchiness	Ls' sensitivity, e.g. in the area of personal description

3.4 *General task descriptors*	Ways of defining, characterising, classifying tasks
Genre	A well-established exercise type
Describe and arrange	L1 describes an arrangement of objects/ people, and L2 draws or recreates it in some way
Find the differences	Ls find differences between similar pictures
Grid completion	Filling in a table/grid from information given
Information gap	Task based on some Ls possessing information which is passed to other Ls who do not have it

Appendix 1   (*Continued*)

General task descriptors	Ways of defining, characterising, classifying tasks
Jigsaw	Information gap task where different Ls have different information. When all information is shared with all Ls, the 'jigsaw' is complete
Mirror exercise	Exercise in which Ls mimic the behaviour/actions of a partner
Picture dictation	T describes a picture at dictation speed and Ls draw it
Projection exercise	Ls project aspects of themselves into the persona of another
Quiz	
Reflexive description	Describing oneself
Role play	
Running dictation	Technique in which class members run to a text pinned on a notice board, read parts of it, then run back and dictate what they have read to a classmate
Type	Task specified in terms of what activities are involved, but not forming a well-established genre (as the ones under 'genre' above)
Text based	Task based on a text
Movement oriented	Task with lots of moving around involved
Drawing	
Scenario	Task specified in terms of the real world situation it is centred upon. E.g. 'meeting someone at an airport'
Airport	Meeting someone at an airport
Crime	Describing the perpetrator of a crime
Describe classmate	
Missing person	
Film making	Casting for a film
Framework	The general 'shape' of a task, potentially involving a bundle of parameters: e.g. description of stages, procedures involved, possible class configurations, possible outcomes

PPP	Presentation → practice → production sequence

3.5 Task components	**Various aspects/component parts of tasks**
3.5.1 Logistics	**Associated with the 'mechanics' of utilising a task**
Logistics	Composite of everything concerned with the organisation of a task: what happens, when it happens, who does what, etc.
Classroom geography	Anything to do with class layout, where people stand, sit, etc.
Number	All 'how many' issues. E.g. how many photos are needed in a task
Rules	What Ls are allowed to do/not do in the task
Configuration	Classroom organisational patterns, as exemplified below
Groupwork	
Individual	Ls work alone
Triads	Ls work in threes
Pairwork	
Whole class	Ls work in plenary, as a class
Role swapping	e.g. stage where Ls who question and those who answer swap roles
Regrouping	Procedure whereby Ls form new groups, e.g. to describe what has been done in an earlier group
Grouping criterion	Criterion used to put Ls into groups
Timing	All matters to do with length of activities, stages
Talk duration	How long Ls talk to each other
Prerequisite(s)	Things T needs to do/obtain before the task is done in class
Props	Items required by T in order to use the task
Cards	
Cassette recorder	
Dictionary	

Appendix 1   (*Continued*)

Task components	Various aspects/component parts of tasks
Drawing	T draws on blackboard, or Ls on paper
Magazine	
Mirror	
Music	
Photocopier	
Photos	
Picture	
Poster	
Video	
Place	Where the task fits into the larger teaching context, or a stage in the task as a whole
Fiddly bits	Little details, like cutting up pieces of paper, using blue tack, etc.

3.5.2 Task stages	The stages Ds themselves identify within a task
Stage	One identifiable (usually self-contained) part of a task
Preparation	Any task seen as preparatory to the main activity
Demonstration	T demonstrates what is to be done
Language preparation	T provides preparation in language to be used in task
Scene setting	Specifically contextualising a scenario
Setting up	Task preparation, usually focused on the logistics of what will happen
Warm-up	A 'dry run' going through the main activities within the task
Revision	Going over already covered work in preparation for the task
Main activity	The core of the task in which learners produce (in the sense of the PPP model) language
Information exchange	Ls exchange information, often in pairs or groups

Production	Stage at which a quantity of production work takes place
Follow-up	Either in class or for homework
Final plenary	
Communicative checking	Checking L output in terms of whether message has got across, task has been fulfilled, rather than for linguistic correctness
Feedback	Ls are given feedback on their performance
Report back	Ls report to class on findings, usually in plenary

3.5.3 Task content	**A rather loose category, covering various aspects of task content**
Purpose	Reason for undertaking a task
Activity	A set of actions which forms a discrete part of a task (or stage thereof). Distinct from 'procedure' which is used only in relation to design processes
L action	The actions an L undertakes at a given point
T action	The actions a T undertakes at a given point
Check understanding	T checks comprehension
Language supply	T action of providing language
Error correction	T corrects language mistakes
Facilitating	T provides assistance in a variety of ways
TL check	T checks that Ls use the target language (TL) and not their L1
Describee	Who is to be described in the task
Classmate	
Family member	
Famous person	
Known person	Someone the Ls know
Persona	Someone an L pretends to be
Self	
Unusual person	
Imaginary person	

Appendix 1   (*Continued*)

Task content	A rather loose category, covering various aspects of task content
Descriptive parameters	Areas the D decides should be described in the task
Physical	
Character	
Input	What Ls are given or told – by the teacher, on the WS on by some other 'input carrier' (see below)
Input carrier	The medium that contains the input
Corpus	Ls use a language corpus as input carrier
Text	
Pictures	
Tape	
Language content	Language that it is predicted will be used in the task
Grammar	
Pronunciation	
Questions	
Register	
Vocabulary	
Outcome	What is produced at the end of a task in terms of a non-linguistic end product
Output	What is produced at the end of a task in linguistic terms
Output medium	Medium/form in which output is required (e.g. in writing, as an email, etc.)
Propositional content	What is talked about, in non-linguistic terms

3.5.4 Participant roles	To do with the various roles Ls may be required to fulfil during the task
L role	Role a given L follows in a task
Information recipient	L who listens to/reads the person description
Scribe	The idea of having one person in the group to write things down
Interaction pattern	All discussion about who talks to whom

3.6 Design process related	Codes associated with the way Ds work
3.6.1 Modi operandi	To do with the D's preferred work habits
Computer working	D likes to work at a computer
Quiet think	D wants to stop and think without verbalising
Silent reading	D reads materials (usually the brief) silently
Work room	Location in which the D wants to work

3.6.2 Control	
State of play	Metacomment by Ds on where in the design process they are
Done	D's statement of what has already (or just) been done
Next	D's statement of what will be done next
To be done	D's statement of what is left to do, or needs to be done at some future point
Doing	D's statement of what is in the process of being done

3.6.3 Issue related	A miscellany of codes associated with problematic issues raised by Ds
Issue	A problem of any kind
Blackboard writing	Issues to do with problems of writing on blackboard
British/American	Which linguistic norms should be used, British or American?
Cultural sensitivity	Issues to do with sensitivities of certain learner groups, related to their cultural background
Data collection	How Ds can get information on how the function of describing people is usually expounded
Differing levels	The class has different L levels within it
Easy resolution	The task can be done too easily
Gender	Ensuring equal gender treatment during the task

Appendix 1 *(Continued)*

Issue related	A miscellany of codes associated with problematic issues raised by Ds
Group size	The group is too large for some activities
Ignorance of situation	Fact that D is given very little information about Ls' context
Inaccurate language	Issue of whether task will lead to errors in performance, and what to do about this
L1 use	Problem of Ls using L1 instead of target language
L attendance	Whether or not Ls will turn up for class
L copying	Issue that Ls cheat by saying what another L has told them
Physical similarities	Fact that in some nationalities Ls look very alike, which makes physical description of people difficult
Props availability	Whether the desired props will in fact be available
Solution	Solution to an issue
T ability	Whether T in a given context will have the ability to handle a suggested task
T choice	The T is left to decide what course of action to take, i.e. an activity is given as optional in TN
T familiarity	Whether a T is familiar or not with a particular task or activity type
T proclivity	Whether T is likely to want to undertake a given task/activity
Wouldn't do	Expression of D's opinion that the task required is one that he or she would never use

3.6.4 Design procedures	Related to procedures undertaken by a D in the course of designing
Procedure	The term is reserved for activities undertaken by designers
Alternative	An alternative is considered to something already proposed

Brainstorm	D brainstorms (considering possible tasks, etc.). Not used to refer to a brainstorming activity which a D may envisage Ls doing in class
Condition	Occurring in <u>identify condition</u>, which are 'it depends on' statements
Dry run	Procedure of trying out a task before class use
Outsider input	Getting an outsider, peer or spouse, etc., to give feedback
Plagiarising	Taking materials from elsewhere (e.g. published textbooks)
Real world language	Related to the procedure of thinking about what linguistic items would be used in a real world situation
Real world situation	Related to the procedure of thinking about what real world situations the target function occurs in
Repertoire	D's repertoire of known/tried activities, tasks, techniques
Reviewing	Related to the procedure of going over task (e.g. next day) before final use
Taskification	Related to the procedure of thinking of a real world situation and converting it into a task fit for class use
Rumination	Pondering a task between draft and final version
Source	Where a task/idea comes from

3.6.5 TB/WS related	Many of the codes on this schedule are used in relation to TB/WS design. Only those confined to that use are listed below
TN/WS format	To do with the appearance of TN/WS
Title	Title for the task
TN introduction	Introductory section of TN dealing with issues such as task aim, props involved, etc.
TN aim	Description in TN of task aim
TN/WS labelling	Decisions on how to label various parts of the TN/WS

Appendix 1   (*Continued*)

TB/WS related	Many of the codes on this schedule are used in relation to TB/WS design. Only those confined to that use are listed below
TN/WS language	Issues to do with how to word notions in the TN/WS (i.e. the best means of expression)

3.6.6 Other	
Non-design activity	E.g. solving the anagram given to practise concurrent verbalisation
End	Design procedure finishes
NWC	Not worth coding

Appendix 2: Example of ATLAS.ti Coding

The example below is taken from D1's *Explore*. The extract corresponds to lines (b) to (d) of the action box summary found in Figure 4.2 on p. 61. The codes shown on the right appear in different colours on the screen, which makes them easy to distinguish. The vertical lines to the left of the codes indicate the portion of the text that is being coded. Clicking on one of these codes highlights the relevant text portion, which makes it easy to identify. ATLAS.ti provides means of displaying collected examples (or 'quotations' as they are called) of the same code. Other much more sophisticated operations are also possible. In this example the codes have been modified slightly, in the interests of clarity.

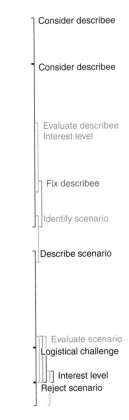

So the sort of thing I am thinking of might be – Describe your ideal boyfriend, girlfriend, husband, wife or something, the ideal film star, the ideal bank manager, the ideal doctor something like that so that we are, we might turn that around and say – your least ideal person if you like, if you can think of it that way, the kind of doctor you wouldn't like to have to go and see, or the kind of bank manager you wouldn't like to have to go and see. That would give more variety, more range of things but at the same time would also I think be more fun as well because describing what you don't like is often much more interesting and would probably be funnier than describing what you really do like. So that's what I'd be going for, it would be something like that. That would be essentially what we would be doing describing ideal or least ideal. It would depend also on the context if we wanted to give it a more intellectual context it might be, we might think of it in terms of sort of ideas about genetic engineering where you need to go along to the sperm bank and set down the requirements what you want for the father of the child I suppose we would have to keep it sort of gender neutral, we would have to as far as it could be gender neutral in a context like that. You would have to have one where, you know, imagine you could choose the egg as well if it was man. But I think that's probably making it a bit more, a bit too complicated, a bit more complicated than it needs to be, although it might be fun in some situations. So we're describing these sorts of people, ideal or least ideal.

Consider describee

Consider describee

Evaluate describee
Interest level

Fix describee

Identify scenario

Describe scenario

Evaluate scenario
Logistical challenge

Interest level
Reject scenario

161

Appendix 3: Example of an Action Box Sequence

This sequence is taken from D13's protocol, and the beginning of his *Instantiate*. It covers the microstage <u>develop framework</u>. The sequence does not contain any examples of the 'Result' box being filled in. This is only filled in when it is necessary to indicate a causal effect between boxes which would otherwise be missed – for example where a decision made leads to a subsequent course of action (e.g. five boxes later).

10	*Instantiate*	*Develop framework*
Operator	Consider	
Operand	WS	
Specification	Poster	
Subsidiary	Philosophise	
Result		
Notes	He likes learners to do their own drawings, and to create for themselves as much of the WS as possible	

11	*Instantiate*	*Develop framework*
Operator	Identify	
Operand	Stage	
Specification	Main activity	
Subsidiary		
Result		
Notes		

12	*Instantiate*	*Develop framework*
Operator	Fix	
Operand	Framework	
Specification	Stages: preparation: demonstration; main activity; configuration: pairwork	
Subsidiary	State of play: next	

Result	
Notes	His design is at this stage very coherent. He establishes the task framework before working on individual stages

13	*Instantiate*	*Develop framework*
Operator	Evaluate	
Operand	Framework	
Specification	Positive	
Subsidiary		
Result		
Notes	The framework, he says, provides 'a reasonable enough sequence'	

Appendix 4: Decisions Made by the End of *Analyse*

To exemplify how Figure A.4 below is to be read: it shows that D2 first fixes what task type to develop, and that it should be one where there is differential information distribution throughout the class. The reason for this decision is that the required task needs to have interactivity. He then decides on the configuration to use – groupwork – the reason being that there is restricted time available for practice. Decisions that take designers forward into their *Analyse* stage appear in bold. In D2's case it is the choice of a scenario – a game which involves identifying a class member. How he arrives at that scenario is not stated. Wherever possible, items in this figure are described in the terminology used for coding (found in Appendix 1).

For D14 the referent <u>type</u> is put in brackets because (as discussed in note 1 of Chapter 5), she establishes <u>type</u> in only the vaguest of ways.

Designer	What is fixed	Details	Basis on which decision made
D1	type	non-present describee	nature of target function
	type	involving lengthy description	nature of target function + task type
	type	**non-present describee + involving lengthy description**	**as above**
D2	type	differential information	need for interactivity
	configuration	groupwork	time available
	scenario	**game identifying class member**	**?**
D3	type	reason for speaking	belief
	unclear		
D4	contextual properties	nationality, age, social class	personal experience
	type	'neutral' situation	chosen recipient (materials writer)
	scenario	**airport**	**repertoire**

D5	type	differential information	design time available/ repertoire/nature of target function
	configuration	pairwork	nature of skill area
	props	**photos**	**?**
D6	type	meaningful, self-revelatory	belief
	genre	**projection exercise**	**repertoire**
D7	recipient	materials writer	personal experience
	procedure	to note important points	belief
	scenario	**airport**	**repertoire**
D8	**type**	**motivational, and problem-solving element**	**belief**
D10	stage	feedback	time available
	configuration	pairwork or triads	need for interactivity
	stage	**demonstration**	**?**
D11	type	activity involving moving around	need for interactivity
	contextual property	togetherness	ad hoc
	genre	role play	nature of target function
	scenario	**crime**	**ad hoc/repertoire**
D12	genre	information gap	repertoire
	props	photos	repertoire
	configuration	pairwork	need to work at different levels
	type	differential information	belief
	scenario	**missing person**	**repertoire**
D13	configuration	pairwork	belief (easy to manage)
	type	differential information	?
	scenario	**missing person**	**repertoire**
D14	[type	based on reading or looking at picture	nature of skill area]
	stage	**warm-up**	**?**

Figure A.4   *(Continued)*

D15	contextual properties	nationality, age, teacher, gender proportion, language knowledge	personal experience
	language content		established during design
	stage	**revision**	**?**
D16	Contextual properties	language knowledge	personal experience
	descriptive parameter		established during design
	stage	**revision**	**?**
D17	**type**	**blackboard drawing**	**?**

Figure A.4   <u>Fix</u> codes appearing by the end of the *Analyse* stage

Appendix 5: Some Designers Philosophise

These pieces of wisdom are taken from protocol items coded <u>philosophise</u> or <u>identify procedure</u>. They are loosely divided into sections, very roughly following through the design process stage by stage. Each section is introduced by a few comments (given in italics).

The design process in general

D3 has a lot to say in his protocol about the design process in general, and well captures (in Quotations 1, 2 and 3) the two sides of the creative act – 'the red hot' inspirational part and the more mundane, tedious hard slog. In Quotation 4 he also touches on that theme, while clarifying the dangers of a DF strategy. A further dichotomy – between the 'scientific' and 'artistic' sides of task design – is mentioned by D6 in Quotation 5. Finally, D13 reminds us that the reality of task design involves working quickly and in less than ideal circumstances (Quotation 6).

1. For me there's a typical stage which I've just reached where the light bulb goes on and you have this world-shattering idea and there's a rather painful bit when you realise that for some perfectly simple reason it will never work and something awful will go wrong with it and it needs more thought before it'll actually work. X [*a colleague of the designer*] is very good at this sort of crack detecting. She'll look at my most brilliant ideas and explain patiently why they'll never actually work in a class. (D3)
2. I'm doing a sort of sharpening pencils thing at the moment which is making it all look neater and putting in dots and numbers and generally messing about. One does this quite often. I think it's just a matter of backing off from the red hot creative intensity. (D3)
3. The thing that strikes me . . . is that the idea is easy and the mechanics are difficult. A lot of the work in doing something like this is, as any experienced teacher will know, getting the mechanics right so that people are in the right place at the right time and nobody's not doing anything. (D3)
4. I see that by this stage I've got firmly committed to this task and I've no interest whatever in pursuing it, but to abandon it means a whole lot more work, and I don't want to do it. I want to make this one work . . . the last thing I want is to back off from what seems to me a fertile idea, because I think the earlier stage is quite painful – the business of floating around in a void trying to get something that'll work. Once you've got hold of something there's a tremendous surge forward and you don't want to get off that road. It's very hard abandoning something and starting again. (D3)
5. It is the usual conflict between a semi-scientific input model from a corpus and putting the students in situations where they actually want certain

things and you then supply them. Is there a way of perhaps marrying the two? I don't know. (D6)

6. The other thing I am conscious of is that I am doing this very quickly and although I am also conscious that I am running on grooved lines – I have done this kind of thing before – it doesn't mean that what I am doing here is perfect or even as perfect as I want it to be. I am very conscious that if I sit down in an evening as a teacher I don't want to spend all evening preparing tasks or designing tasks. I want to produce something that is valid, or what I think is valid and enjoyable for the class in as short a time as possible. But there is a balance. Why I am not going really to town on this, I am not doing the best I could possibly do is because this is how I would probably do it if I was sitting down in an evening...so I've just realised why am I hurrying through this. I mean that this is actually, if I have got three or four lessons to prepare for the next day and I am thinking I want to put my own tasks in, I...wouldn't spend all evening doing it. (D13)

Starting points

A major theme of Chapter 5 is what designers choose to highlight in the early stages of design, and what they identify as their starting points (even though, as we see in Chapter 5, they may not always do what they say they will do). In Quotations 7 and 8 we find evidence of the view that tasks should be purposeful, and involve language use to some communicative end. As Chapter 5 also shows, the strategy of identifying real world situations (and then taskifying one of them) is a common one, and is represented here in Quotations 9–12. But Quotations 13 and 14 illustrate that there are other concerns to be addressed, and these may suggest slightly different approaches.

7. Right OK well I've got the basic idea of it and what I'd now be looking for or thinking about doing is thinking of some sort of purpose the activity might have. (D1)

8. So I give them a reason for talking about people. (D3)

9. I may just think of a setting, a scenario of some sort where describing people is going to be a necessary or a plausible thing to do. I think that's the starting point – to try and find some context where describing people is going to be necessary. Yeh I'm actually thinking back and thinking through to some of the stuff that I've done and some material I just wrote. (D7)

10. Right so the starting point really needs to be a natural situation in which describing people would actually occur. There would be a genuine communicative reason for doing it and that should in turn provide the problem solving dimension or the fun aspect or something like that, or provide some kind of interactive meat for the whole thing. (D8)

11. So a situation where it would be natural to describe people, including character, right not just physical appearance, but at the same time bearing in mind the level of these learners. (D8)

12. Let's see now, you begin with an input of some kind on describing people. What would be the natural thing to say? They might talk, but why, why compare the different characteristics of people in this way? Why look at whether they are tall or they're short? (D8)

13. Let's just think now of any way of doing it. You don't necessarily need a real life communicative reason to do it as long as it's enjoyable in the classroom and the language use is natural. (D8)

14. I am going to start off by thinking about the class a little bit. Personally I like them to be working in pairs because I find that is an easy thing to manage but I also don't mind mixing activities. But I actually like pairwork because I think people can work, be at different levels within pairwork. So I am probably going to do a pairwork activity from that angle. And I have got to think up a way of getting some kind of information gap, which is going to use the language of describing people. In other words where one person is describing someone possibly and the other has to find out information about the person. But I want to try and put it into some kind of situation which is relevant to them or at least has a real life world type situation which they might conceivably use the language in. (D13)

Using repertoire

The use of repertoire is a recurrent theme in this study. The following quotations illustrate three designers frankly acknowledging the role of what might politely termed repertoire (sometimes, less politely, as a form of plagiarism!). But, as two quotations in particular (16 and 20) suggest, the ideas of others are used as a springboard for the production of something that, hopefully at least, will end up being 'new and revolutionary'. As it happens, the designers cited here are all NS/Ts. But as we discussed in Chapter 5, repertoire certainly also plays an important role in the work of S designers.

15. Let's look at describing people and again in my head I'm thinking of a book called Cambridge English Course which has a lot of materials on this area and no doubt I can draw on some of that material just as a start. (D12)

16. Also when I first saw describing people I immediately think of other published materials I am familiar with so it is not going to be something I do from scratch. I can draw on those materials for ideas and for information gap activities or something like that. (D12)

17. OK what I am thinking about now actually is some of the tasks that I have done in the past already and I have got one particular one in mind that I might want to use. (D13)

18. OK now probably at this stage I would probably have a look through a couple of books and find a form, like a missing person form or something similar and rip it off and probably do it on the computer so it is more realistic. (D13)

19. OK so my first thought is definitely I will be thinking about something I have already done in the past. I am going to base the activity on something I have done or possibly which in itself is an amalgam of things that I have seen from bits and bobs from different books. (D13)

20. I guess I am going to try put together ideas that I have already used in some new way or put together ideas that I have seen in books, in resources elsewhere and combine them in my own way. That's how I usually do these sort of things. And maybe something new and revolutionary will turn up in the process. (D16)

Language content

As is mentioned in Chapter 6, there are considerable variations in the degree of attention different designers give to the language content of their tasks. D7 is the designer who perhaps shows the greatest degree of interest in this topic. Here are three of his thoughts on the subject. In Quotations 21 and 22 he makes two suggestions about how 'objective' data on language use might be collected, and in 23 he is thinking about the sequencing of utterances (a point mentioned on p. 102 in relation to him).

21. I suppose this [*the point of establishing language content*] is where a corpus of some sort would be useful to go along to and try and get some . . . real data of how people really use the language. But we'll have to use our intuition instead. (D7)
22. This is where some real data would be useful to see how people really describe. It would be very nice actually to just get some photographs of people and show them round and say to some friends or colleagues 'how would you describe this person?' and see what comes out, because what I'm doing at the moment is sort of scraping around in my head thinking what would I say, whereas in fact I would probably say something completely different from what I think I would say. (D7)
23. And actually what's interesting about these of course is that they build together, don't they, into sequences. So 'He's an interesting sort of person', and 'He's got a wonderful sense of humour' would go together . . . 'He doesn't laugh very much', 'He's a very serious person'. Interesting isn't it how we string those things together, it's a bit blunt to say about somebody 'He's interesting.' You tend to add a bit more on to that. (D7)

Design in full spate

This section contains a collection of points on a variety of matters. In 24, D1 proclaims the value of demonstration in class. Then follows a series of quotations from D5, whose protocol is full of interesting thoughts on the specifics of task design. In Quotation 25 he is articulating why reviewing the brief is such an important activity, and in 26 he expresses possibly somewhat unfashionable (though doubtless justifiable) views about pairwork. He also (27) makes a point about timing, observed by a number of designers. Not many of the designers on the other hand attempt humour in their tasks, and in 28 D1 explains why. The sentiments about technology expressed (by D5 again) in Quotation 29 will doubtless ring true for many readers.

24. It's always a good idea to do that [*choose a pair to demonstrate an activity*] I find, because even if you explain an activity you can't be sure that everybody has understood it. So it is always best to get as close to the actual activity as possible by getting one pair to demonstrate; and it may throw up certain problems and so that will help. [*reading back*] . . . 'Demonstrate the activity.' (D1)
25. *Int*: Are you just reading the brief at this moment?
     D5: Yeah I'm just making sure that I haven't missed anything cos sometimes I read things too quickly and miss out a crucial fact so you want to check as much as possible. . . . (D5)

26. A big problem with a lot of this pairwork and groupwork is keeping the class together and what to do if one group or pair finishes before everybody else. It seems to me on the whole a lot of pairwork is pretty catastrophic... and I must say that in a couple of decades of observing classes I don't think I've ever seen it done – ever, not even once really – ideally... meaning that everybody's... on task and working and finishing at more or less the same time. On the whole they don't work like that, and I have three kids of my own and they've all done pairwork in the learning of French and German... and it's clearly a complete waste of time after the first few minutes. Also I think they tend to resent having very weak partners with them which was the way their school organised it. I remember one of my kids saying that after about half a term of this, that you know he wasn't paid for being the teacher and that... he was learning nothing from it. Whereas again of course the teacher's ideology here is, it tends to be that, you know, pupils are all benevolent and are all dying to help each other. (D5)

27. Now given that I always underestimate the amount of time needed for things, 20 minutes probably about right, it's probably going to take 30 at the end of the day. (D5)

28. You might add a little bit of humour in it although humour is always a problem with English because you never know how well it's going to travel. (D1)

29. It's little things like this [*telling the learners in what sequence to look at the photos*] that foul things up very often. Yes, like having a video and the video doesn't work. You know you can have all wonderful activities constructed around it but unless you've checked that your video has not corrupted.... It was alas the fate of a conference I went to recently when people had come from all over the... world for this thing, and you know, the boss of the organization comes on with his video and it was corrupted and he hadn't looked at it for something like 8 months so what do you expect? It's [*a question*] I think quite often of getting the details right. (D5)

Writing teacher instructions/TN/WS

In Chapter 6 we noted how many designers use the writing of TN/WS as a means of instantiating their tasks. Quotations 30–32 below well express the revisionary and developmental value of WS/TN writing. Quotations 33–35 deal with questions related to the language and content of TNs/WSs, matters which D1 in particular has strong views on. Among the other issues raised in this section are questions of location – where particular pieces of information are best placed (Quotations 36 and 37). The final quotations, 40 and 41, capture a major problem with WS/TN writing, and one which non-specialists often find especially perplexing – how to describe complex and detailed classroom procedures, particularly in such a way that another teacher will be able to use them.

30. It's amazing how writing teacher's notes helps to clarify thinking. Because you actually have to sort of think your way through doing it, and... things that seemed a good idea in the first place turn out not to be. (D1)

31. Now I'm just writing out instructions for doing this as I would write them out for a teacher and hoping that this will show up any weak links or things that... wouldn't work. (D3)

32. It's quite often at this stage when you actually start writing the language itself that I think you might find some sort of washback effect that might lead you to revise some of the language that I'd already mentioned – adjectives and verbal structures and whatever. But when you actually came down to it you might find good heavens you know such and such a bit of language is actually very useful, and in that case you know anybody sensible would … not say 'oh too bad, I've already, I've already decided what language I'm going to choose'. And what you would do is say 'well if it's useful in a description it clearly justifies inclusion' and we would then go back [*and try and fit it in somehow*]. (D5)

33. Now I tend to give my teachers' notes in direct speech. Is it direct? Yes, direct speech. So rather than saying 'ask a student whether such and such' I will, say 'ask a student "you, do this"'; so you actually give the actual sentence that the teacher would use. So instead of saying 'Ask a student what his or her ideal boyfriend or girlfriend is like, would be like', which would be the sort of embedded form, you say – 'ask what would your ideal boyfriend, girlfriend be like?' The reason for this is first of all you avoid a lot of embedding which can make the language more complex. The other thing is that it, it actually provides the teacher with the actual words to use which in some cases may be important to the teachers who want to use English in the classroom but are not quite sure of what they should actually say, and so by giving them the actual sentence to say you will make the task a lot easier. On the other hand [*this*] can sound a bit patronizing as well to teachers whose language is obviously very good. But again it's a toss up between which teacher you go for. My inclination … is to go for the weaker teacher on the basis that they are the ones who need the help and can't do it without. (D1)

34. It helps to keep the students' rubric as simple as possible. (D1)

35. And I tend to go for the recipe book myself on the basis that the other teachers can get by and help themselves, whereas the teacher who needs the recipe book can't, and so we'll go for that approach. (D1)

36. But quite frankly if this is part of a book, that sort of stuff has to go into the introduction because it is general, it is not just applicable to this particular exercise. But … the problem is that people don't read introductions. (D6)

37. But generally I find it easier to have the bones of the task with the students as well, and then the teachers' notes are an expansion of that. (D1)

38. I see a dreaded word worksheet here. I hate doing worksheets. What I like best is activities where you've got a fairly short instruction and that generates the activity without my having to do extra work, doing pictures or checklists or whatever. (D3)

39. Right it's also amazing how normally you end up having to cut things rather than add things. (D1)

40. It is very difficult to set up precise instructions for doing an activity like this, for somebody who doesn't know how to do it. It's very difficult to spell it out, exactly what needs to be done. … It's a great problem actually. It's all very clear in your head but making it clear to other people isn't at all easy. (D7)

41. Notes for another teacher. OK it is kind of difficult as you get used to your own sort of scheme of doing things. (D11)

Late modifications to tasks

Designers are well aware that the design process does not stop after the initial creation of a task, and the writing of the TN and WS. Further revision will occur either after piloting the task in a class (Quotations 42 and 43) or following a period of rumination (Quotations 44–46).

42. Now, generally I find with tasks that the first draft doesn't work very well. Well, you find out whether it works or not and if it works, what you need to do to revise it. So you might need to change the categories, find that you need a bit more interest, or find that students need a bit more preparation, or something like that. But the only way to find that out is to actually use it in the class. (D1)

43. *Int*: Would you anticipate it changing much or you doing much more design work?
    D4: I think it would change enormously once I'd taught it. (D4)

44. *D4*: I think where it would really change is once I'd got the pikkies in.
    Int: Right basically what I'm trying to judge here is would it be me sitting here just watching you typing or will some design work happen?
    D4: Oh well something else happens. OK well now I think probably not because if it does it will happen after I've gone out and dug the garden which is what I will do now or something. I'll put it away OK. I'll put it away probably and come back to it the next day and have a look at it. But I would probably put it into a neater form first. But now I know roughly what I'm going to do. (D4)

45. OK I suppose I should do it again but no I'd rather think about it overnight I think. (D4)

46. In real life terms this is too close to the write up to be a sensible time to revise that. I would normally do it tomorrow morning . . . I am too close to the text [*at present*] and the two main reasons [*for revision*] are obviously language, to pull out nonsense in the language but . . . I also need to really check out the choreography of how this lesson develops . . . which might mean a complete rewrite. (D6)

Appendix 6: The Designers' Tasks

The final task of each designer has been standardised, and shortened so that all important material could be put on one side of A4. See Chapter 8 for discussion on the production of these task summaries, which was done by Virginia Samuda.

Designer D1's task

Title.   Ideal people.

Overview.   The task involves exchanging opinions about the characteristics of the ideal/least ideal best friend, partner, doctor, teacher.

Stages.

1. Students receive a list of people: (A) best friend; (B) husband/wife; (C) doctor or teacher. Individually, students make notes on characteristics (physical appearance and personality) to describe their idea of: (a) the most ideal person in each category and (b) the least ideal person in each category.
2. Students form pairs and exchange their ideas on category A.
3. Students form new pairs and exchange ideas on category B.
4. Students form new pairs and exchange ideas on category C.
5. One pair from each category present their ideas to the rest of the class.

Materials required.   Worksheet for each student.

Worksheet.

1a   Look at this list of people
    A   Best friend
    B   Husband/wife
    C   Doctor or teacher

1b   What would your ideal and least ideal person in each category be like? Put down some ideas. Describe their physical appearance and character.

2a   Work in pairs. Take the first category:
    Student A: Tell your partner about your ideal and least ideal best friend.
    Example: My ideal best friend would be ... S/he would have....
    Student B: Ask Student A questions to get some more details.

2b   Reverse roles and repeat.
3.   Find a new partner and discuss your ideas for the second category. Reverse roles and repeat.
4.   Find a new partner and discuss your ideas for the third category. Reverse roles and repeat.

Designer D2's task

Overview.   The task involves agreeing on a cast list for a play.

Stages.

1. The class is divided into 'producers' and 'theatrical agents'. Working in groups of three: the 'producers' receive the outline of a play and a list of characters, with details about age, appearance and personality, and they have to describe in more detail the characteristics of each character on their worksheet; the 'theatrical agents' receive a list of actors, with details about age, appearance, personality and the kinds of roles each actor typically plays. They have to describe in more detail the characteristics of each actor on their worksheets.
2. Students regroup; each 'producer' group gets together with a 'theatrical agent' group to exchange information on roles and actors available, and together they have to agree on a cast list for the play. Outcome: Cast list.
3. The class comes together and all groups compare their cast lists and explain why they chose the actors they did.

Materials required.   Student worksheets.

Worksheets.

Producers

Step 1:   You are concerned with producing a play. Here is a list of the roles. Describe in more detail the characteristics of each role.

Step 2:   Go to a theatrical agent. The agent has a list of actors. Describe to the agent the kinds of actors you need. Match his/her list with your requirements.

Aim: To produce a suitable cast list for your play.

Character	Age	Appearance	Job	Personality
Grandma	66			
Mother	41			
Father	43			
Daughter	18			
Son	17			
Girlfriend	17			
Cousin	20			

Theatrical agents

Step 1:   You are an agent for actors. You have the following actors on your list. Add details to the list, e.g. names, typical roles that they play.

Step 2:   You are approached by a producer who wishes to cast a play. From your list of actors, suggest ones which match his/her requirements.

Aim: To agree a suitable cast list for the play.

Actor	Age	Appearance	Personality	Typical Role
F				
M				
M				
F				
F				
F				
M				
M				
F				
M				

Designer D3's task

Overview.   The task involves acting out, observing and describing the appearance and behaviour of other people.

Preparation.   A place for students to go outside the classroom; a way for them to change clothes (the teacher brings in some odd things – raincoats, anoraks, Wellingtons ...); three cassette recorders.

Stages.

1. Two students go out of the room; the rest divide into three groups of four or so. The two students who have gone out should change clothes and decide on ways of behaving, chosen from a list.
2. The two students enter in turn, stay in the room for one minute, behave in a particular way, and go out again.
3. Each group then discusses what they saw. (They should do this in English.) Their aim is to come up with an agreed description of each person's appearance and behaviour. One member of each group makes brief notes recording the group's decisions.
4. Each group leader records on cassette his/her group's description.
5. Finally the three recordings are played to the whole class, including the two who were sent out (now allowed back in).

Materials required.   Clothing; a list of ways of behaving for the pair leaving the room; three cassette recorders.

Designer D4's task

Title.   At the airport.

Overview.   The task involves describing people so that they can be recognised on arrival at the airport.

Stages.

1. Students work in groups of three. Each group is going to meet somebody they do not know at the airport. Their friends are meeting somebody off a different airline at a different airport and they have to describe the arriving person so that they can be recognised when they arrive. Each group is given a different full-length photo to describe.
2. Students regroup so that each person has a partner from another group. They exchange descriptions of the person they are going to meet.
3. Each person in the group returns to their own group and exchanges the information they received.
4. Reminding the class that there are many other people on this flight, not just the ones they are meeting, the teacher announces the flight arrival, holds up a photo and walks across the room. The aim is to shout out the name before the teacher reaches the other side. The group which guesses the quickest is the winner. (Note: the teacher first holds up a picture someone who is not being met). The teacher repeats this process with all the other photos.

Materials required. Ten [very large] full-length photos of different people. Each photo is named. There is a range of photos, from simple to more difficult.

Designer D5's task

Overview. The task involves (a) listening to descriptions of different people and identifying them in photographs and (b) finding differences between two pictures.

Stages.

1. The teacher attaches eight large photos of different people to the blackboard and labels them A to H. S/he describes each photo in random order, using three sentences for each one. Students write down the letter of the appropriate photo after each description.
2. Students work in pairs, sitting opposite each other. Each pair receives an envelope with six pairs of photographs clipped together inside. Each photo in each pair has a number on the back 1 to 6. Starting with the first pair of photos, students find three differences between them, without showing their pictures to each other. Students write down the differences that they find, and move on to the next pair of photos.
3. Pairs of students read aloud the first difference for photo 1. A different pair reads out the second difference and so on. The same procedure for the next five pairs of photos.

Materials required. Eight large photos of different people, labelled A to H; envelopes with six pairs of photos inside: one envelope per pair.

Worksheet/instructions.

> Find 3 differences and write them down.
> Use English.
> You have 6–10 minutes.

Designer D6's task

Title. Who are my classmates?

Overview. The task involves creating and carrying out a questionnaire on various aspects of peoples' appearances.

Preparation. The teacher writes the name of each student in the class on a separate card, and brings to class.

Stages.

1. Students work in groups. Each group prepares 7–10 questions on a specialised area relating to appearance:
   Group 1: how people move (i.e. sit down, stand up, walk, run)
   Group 2: people's dress sense (colour preference, awareness of line, etc.)
   Group 3: people's voices
   Group 4: people's faces
   Group 5: metaphorical (would X make a good waitress/lawyer/space traveller, etc.).
2. When groups are ready, the teacher collects and photocopies questions, distributing a copy to each student.
3. Each student picks a card with someone's name on it.
4. Students work in pairs: using the questionnaire created by the class, Student A interviews Student B about the student whose name B has picked.
5. Repeat the interview with B questioning and A responding.

Materials required.   Cards with students' names; access to a photocopier.

Designer D7's task

Overview.   The task involves looking at pictures of people and building descriptions of them, drawing on sets of descriptive phrases.

Stages.

1. Students form four groups. Each group forms a circle and receives a different list of phrases: Group A: Physical Description; Group B: Character; Group C: Hobbies/Pastimes; Group D: Family Relationships. Within each group, students take it in turns to read out a phrase from their list, focusing on pronunciation.
2. The students regroup so that four new groups contain one (maybe two) members of each old group. Each group receives four pictures of different people. Each group builds up agreed on descriptions of each picture, using one phrase from each of the four sets of characteristics from the previous stage.
3. The descriptions of the four pictures made up by each group can be shared and compared.

Materials required.   One sheet of blank paper per student; four sets of phrases A–D given below (photocopied); four copies of four pictures of different people.

Worksheets. (Sample phrases: others could be added/substituted)

Group A: Physical Description	Group B: Character
She's quite tall, about 1 m 75.	He's got a wonderful sense of humour.
He's not very tall.	He doesn't laugh very much.
She's got long black hair.	He's a very serious person.
He's got short fair hair.	He's an interesting sort of person.
She often wears glasses.	He's a very determined person, he knows exactly what he wants.
She's quite slim, etc. etc. etc.	He can never make his mind up about anything, etc. etc. etc.
Group C: Hobbies/Pastimes	**Group D: Family Relationships**
He likes sailing.	He's married.
He's very keen on swimming/outdoor things.	He isn't married.
He's a workaholic.	He's getting married soon.
He's only interested in his work.	He's living with ...
	He's got two young/teenage/grown-up children.
He collects ...	He hasn't got any children, etc. etc. etc.
He plays a lot of ... etc. etc. etc.	

Designer D8's task

Title. Guess who?

Overview. The task involves playing a card game; the goal is guess the identity of the people depicted on the cards and collect as many cards as possible.

Stages.

1. Working in groups of three or four, students put the cards face down in the centre of the table.
2. Player 1 takes the top card and looks at it <u>without showing it to the other players</u>.
3. The other players in turns ask yes/no questions to find out who the person on the card is. (For example: Is he tall? Is she short? Is he handsome? etc.) The player with the card answers 'yes' or 'no'.
4. The player who guesses correctly is given the card to keep and gets one point. She/he then takes the next card from the pile. The game then continues as before.

NB If a player asks or answers a question in their own language, he/she loses a point.

Materials required.   12 cards with pictures/names of famous people (living or dead). For example: Pope John Paul; Nelson Mandela; Bill Clinton; Gandhi; Queen Elizabeth; Tina Turner; Pavarotti; Bill Gates; sportspeople; names of students and others (e.g. teachers) known to the students, etc. etc. etc.

Designer D10's task

Overview.   The task involves describing a person to someone who does not know him/her.

Stages.

1. Working individually, students think about a person they know well, making notes if they wish.
2 Students work in pairs and take turns to tell their partner about the person they've been thinking about. Student A speaks to Student B; Student B asks any questions they want to know about the person. Reverse roles.

Materials required.   None.

Designer D11's task

Overview.   The task involves (a) taking part in an interview between a detective and a witness to a robbery, and (b) building a profile of a set of criminals from their photographs.

Stages.

1. Students work in pairs. Student A=the detective; Student B=the witness. The 'witnesses' receive a photo of the suspect, which they do not show the detective.
2. The detective prepares questions; the witness studies the photo for one minute.
3. The detective asks questions; the witness responds. At the end of the interview, they compare the description and the photo.
4. Students swap partners.
5. After several turns, students form new pairs. Using all the photographs they build up profiles of each criminal, in pairs, writing a character description and physical description for each one.

Materials required.   A bank of photographs.

Designer D12's task

Title.   Describing people.

Overview.   The task involves describing a classmate to other classmates and guessing the identity of the person being described.

Stages.

1. Each student receives a piece of paper containing the name of another student in the class.
2. Working individually, students think about and note down ways of describing that person.
3. Students imagine they are at a party or a conference and need to describe their person to someone who does not know him/her. They walk around the class, mingling with each other and starting conversations in which they describe their person, without revealing the name. The aim is to speak to as many people as possible – a minimum of four.
4. The teacher brings the class together, inviting students to guess the identities of the people they heard described, and to explain why they thought so.

Materials required. The names of each student in the class written on a separate piece of paper.

Designer D13's task

Overview. The task involves making a missing person poster and taking part in a role-play interview between a policeman and a relative of the missing person.

Stages.

1. Students each receive a poster sheet. Working individually, they draw a picture of someone they know who might have gone missing. They do not show their posters to each other.
2. Students form pairs. A = a policeman. B = a relative of the missing person who phones the police station. 'Policemen' receive a blank report form.
3. Student A uses the report form to ask Student B questions about the missing person and to record the answers. Student B answers the questions based on his/her poster.
4. Students change pairs and reverse roles.

Materials required. Missing person poster sheets; missing person report forms.

Worksheets.

In the box, draw a picture of somebody you know who has gone missing. Do not show your poster to other people.
MISSING   Have you seen this person? If so, please contact (01524) 783642 as soon as possible.

MISSING PERSON REPORT FORM

Work in pairs, sitting back to back. A is the policeman and B is reporting the missing person. A uses the missing persons form and asks B questions about the missing person. B uses his/her poster to answer A's questions. When you finish, change roles.			
Date		Clothes	
Height		Personality	
Colour of eyes		Smoker	
Colour of hair		Distinguishing features	
Build			

Designer D14's task

Overview.   The task involves taking part in a role play of an interview between a journalist and a famous person.

Stages.

1. Students select a photograph of a famous person from a bank of photos displayed by the teacher.
2. Students work in pairs. Student A is the interviewer, Student B is the famous person depicted in the selected photograph, who is to be interviewed. Students have a few minutes for preparation: 'interviewers' prepare questions, 'famous people' make notes on things they could say about themselves.
3. Student A asks questions and Student B answers.
4. Students swap roles with a new partner.

Materials required.   Bank of photographs of famous people, likely to be known by the students.

Worksheet/instructions.

Look at the pictures of famous people that your teacher will show you. Pick the photograph of the person you want to describe. Work in pairs. Student A: You are a journalist about to interview a famous person. Prepare questions to ask. Student B: You are the person in the picture. You are going to be interviewed by a journalist. What can you tell them about yourself? Interview your partner and then change to another pair. When you change partners, change roles: interviewers become interviewees; interviewees become interviewers.

Designer D15's task

Overview.   The task involves (a) developing a bio-data of a person in a picture; (b) describing and identifying pictures of people and (c) playing a game to guess the identity of a famous person by asking questions about him/her.

Stages.

1. Students work in pairs with a pile of 15–20 small pictures. Student A gives a bio-description of the person in the first picture, saying as many things as s/he can about the person, and using five different adjectives in their description. Student B keeps count of the adjectives used, and then repeats as much information as s/he can remember.
2. Students work in groups of four, with several pictures on the table between them. One person describes one of the people in the pictures. Afterwards, the rest of the group guess who it is, using specific questions forms: first, WH-questions only and then Yes/No questions only.
3. Students come together as a whole class. One student chooses someone in the class or a famous person everyone knows, and stands up and describes their person in 30 seconds, without giving his/her name. The first person to guess it puts up their hand and says: Is it . . . ?, scoring a point for correctly guessing.

Materials required.   A bank of pictures of people.

Designer D16's task

Overview.   The task involves (a) playing a 20 Questions game about class members and (b) describing a picture for somebody else to draw.

Stages.

1. In pairs, students play 20 Questions: Student A thinks of a student in the class. Student B ask questions to discover who it is. The answers can only be yes/no. Reverse roles and then change pairs.
2. Students work in pairs. Student A has a picture of Person A and describes it to Student B. Student B listens and draws, but doesn't see the picture.
3. Students reverse roles and repeat with the picture of Person B.
4. Students check results to see if the pictures are the same, and if not, why not.
5. If there is time, students make their own drawings of people to describe to each other.

Materials required.   Two pictures:

PERSON A *Drawing of a tall thin man with very long arms and very long legs long thin face, sticky out ears, curly hair, big nose. Dressed as an athlete: vest, pair of shorts. Very smiley.*	**PERSON B** *Drawing of an average build woman, not too fat or too thin; wearing a skirt, a pair of high-heeled shoes; round face, little ears, long and straight hair; not happy looking, but not unhappy*

Designer D17's task

Overview.   The task involves describing people in a picture.

Stages.

1. The teacher puts up a large picture depicting several people playing sports (or draws a picture on the blackboard).
2. Students work in pairs. Student A (the speaker) describes the people in the picture to Student B (the listener). After the speaker has finished, the listener adds anything the speaker may have missed.
3. The students come together as a whole class and tell what they have found.

Materials required.   A large picture or a blackboard drawing.

Notes

1 Why Study Task Design?

1. The colleague was R. V. White and the workshops were held for the British Schools chain in Italy.
2. The source is the 1997 British Council/British Tourist Authority advice pack entitled <u>Marketing English Language Courses</u>. I am indebted to David Crystal for making this information available. His own estimate is for a lower number.
3. The project, entitled 'Capturing expertise in task design for instruction and assessment', was funded by the ESRC as part of their Cognitive Engineering Initiative (grant No. L127251031). Apart from myself, the researchers on the project were: James Ridgway (School of Education, University of Durham); Tom Ormerod and Catherine Fritz (Department of Psychology, Lancaster University); Virginia Samuda (Department of Linguistics and Modern English Language, Lancaster University).
4. I was awarded a Leverhulme Trust Research Fellowship which ran from September 2000 till August 2001. It was during this time that the major part of the work described in this book was undertaken.
5. In the event the card sort study was not productive and was hence not pursued to conclusion.
6. Details of how to obtain this draft version are given on the Lancaster University Language Teaching Design Procedures Group (LTDPG) website: www.ling.lancs.ac.uk/groups/ltdpg/ltdpg.htm.

2 Some Studies in Expertise

1. Throughout this book we shall follow Schoenfeld and use the term 'control'.

3 Studying Task Designers at Work

1. This description of the Wood Choppers' Ball is taken from Johnson (1996: 37).
2. Following Ericsson & Simon (1978), Smagorinsky distinguishes three levels of verbalisation. The type of verbalisation referred to in this quotation is Level 2 – the type which offers 'explication of thought content'.
3. Perhaps for these textbook writers, like others we know, writing a book together in fact means working separately on one half each, and only bringing the two halves together at the end.
4. An example is <u>financial status</u>. One designer observes that the brief makes no reference to the financial standing of the students, relevant to him because he wants to include descriptions of clothing in his task, and wonders whether differences in earnings between students might be reflected in the way they dress, and hence might lead to embarrassment in discussion.

5. Occasionally there are sections of protocol which simply do not fit into these macrostages. Rather than introduce new labels to handle these isolated cases, they are simply coded as microstages, not associated with any macrostage.

4 A Look at Two Designers

1. Items written in italics and placed in brackets – [] – take the form of notes. They convey information not sufficiently important or common enough in the data to warrant a specific code.
2. The word 'philosophise' is being used throughout in the sense given in Appendix 1. The reader needs to be aware that all code words/phrases bear the specialised meanings given in Appendix 1. Appendix 5 contains selected pieces of 'philosophising' from the designers, including George's thoughts on rubric writing.
3. An alternative way of regarding the structure of this protocol would be to view what is described in this paragraph as part of the preparation phase.
4. It is not entirely clear what Colin means by 'materials'. He is probably referring to the small number of <u>props</u> needed, though it is possible that he may also have in mind the lack of necessity for a long WS and TN.

5 Designing Language Teaching Tasks: Beginnings

1. Figure A.4 in Appendix 4 indicates that D14 does in fact establish <u>type</u> before <u>stage</u>. It is felt justified not to include her decision about <u>type</u> in Figure 5.5 because her established type only gives the vaguest indication of the nature of the activity she is designing.
2. One cannot of course discount the possibility that the shape of a task has been established but not articulated.

6 Designing Language Teaching Tasks: Middles and Ends

1. The summary does not repeat referents. So in (b) 'Explore' stands for 'Explore real world situation B'. The action boxes are based on the protocol of a pilot subject.
2. The <u>alternative</u> code was a difficult one to work with, and while these figures do represent a true difference between the S and NS/T groups, they are not in themselves very reliable. One reason for this was the difficulty in plotting alternatives across macrostage boundaries. For example, a designer might propose a configuration (e.g. pairwork) at an early point during *Instantiate*, but change this to triad work late in the *Write TN* procedure. The danger is that considerations of alternatives like this would be missed.
3. There are of course pedagogic implications here. If the presence of coherence markers does not necessarily imply coherence, then the teaching of these markers will not necessarily result in coherence.
4. The same might be said to hold for some of the other codes associated with control. It is doubtless true that some expressions of <u>state of play</u> and <u>identify procedure</u> are included by helpful designers to provide the

researchers with information, and would not occur in normal, unmonitored design.

5. D13 does in fact return later to the <u>descriptive parameter</u> issue. But this is when his task design is complete and he is questioned by the researcher on some details of its content.

6. Interestingly D2 is one of those designers, discussed on p. 91, who claims he will seek real world situations and 'taskify' one of them. But he does not do this. In his case he does not abandon this proclaimed strategy because he has a ready-made task in his repertoire. His procedure is clearly to start with a favoured genre (jigsaw) and seek to insert within it the *describing people* function.

8 Evaluating and Teaching Task Design

1. The part of Samuda's work reported here was also supported by the Leverhulme Trust's grant.

2. Samuda's work in evaluating the tasks went beyond what is reported on here, in accordance with the aims of further work she is doing in the area.

3. Since there were ten evaluators each making five choices for <u>most</u> and five for <u>least</u> preferred tasks, the total possible nominations for each category is 50. The actual totals (49 and 48) come about because one evaluator made four, not five, nominations for <u>most preferred</u>, while two evaluators did the same for the <u>least preferred</u> category.

4. My thanks to Russell Bowater for his substantial help with the statistical analysis and interpretation of these evaluation findings.

5. Samuda has been exploring this dimension in more detail, as part of work in progress.

6. As noted in Chapter 1, the ESRC project that was the starting point for this research involved production of a draft *Task Design Guide* (Samuda *et al.* 2000). See p. 185 for details of how to obtain Part 1 of this draft version.

References

Ackoff, R. 1979 'The future of operations research is past'. *Journal of Operations Research Society* 30: 93–104.

Alderson, J. C., Nagy, E. & Öveges, E. (eds) 2000 *English Language Education in Hungary, Part 2: Examining Hungarian Learners' Achievements in English* Budapest: The British Council.

Allard, F. & Starkes, J. L. 1991 'Expertise in human motor performance'. In Ericsson, K. A. & Smith, J. (eds) *Towards a General Theory of Expertise* Cambridge: Cambridge University Press, 126–52.

Allwright, R. L. 1998 Entry on 'Theory-then-research/research-then-theory'. In Johnson, K. & Johnson, H. (eds) *Encyclopedic Dictionary of Applied Linguistics* Oxford: Blackwell, 352.

Anderson, J. R. 1983 *The Architecture of Cognition* Cambridge, Mass.: Harvard University Press.

Ball, L. J., Evans, J. St. B. T., Dennis, I. & Ormerod, T. C. 1997 'Problem-solving strategies and expertise in engineering design'. *Thinking and Reasoning* 3(4): 247–70.

Ball, L. J. & Ormerod, T. C. 1995 'Structured and opportunistic processing in design: a critical discussion'. *International Journal of Human–Computer Studies* 43: 131–51.

Bereiter, C. & Scardamalia, M. 1993 *Surpassing Ourselves: an Inquiry into the Nature and Implications of Expertise* Chicago: Open Court.

Berkenkotter, C. 1983 'Decisions and revisions: the planning strategies of a publishing writer'. *College Composition and Communication* 34(2): 156–69.

Bogdan, R. C. & Biklen, S. K. 1992 *Qualitative Research for Education* Boston: Allyn & Bacon.

Breen, M. P. 1987 'Learner contributions to task design'. In Candlin, C. N. & Murphy, D. F. (eds) *Language Learning Tasks* London: Prentice Hall, 23–46.

Brumfit, C. J. 1981 'Notional syllabuses revisited: a response'. *Applied Linguistics* 2(1): 90–2.

Bryman, A. & Burgess, R. G. 1994a 'Developments in qualitative data analysis: an introduction'. In Bryman, A. & Burgess, R. G. (eds) *Analysing Qualitative Data* London: Routledge, 1–17.

Bryman, A. & Burgess, R. G. 1994b (eds) *Analysing Qualitative Data* London: Routledge.

Bygate, M., Skehan, P. & Swain, M 2001 *Researching Pedagogic Tasks* London: Pearson Education.

Candlin, C. N. 1987 'Towards task-based language learning'. In Candlin, C. N. & Murphy, D. F. (eds) *Language Learning Tasks* London: Prentice Hall, 5–22.

Charness, N. 1991 'Expertise in chess: the balance between knowledge and search'. In Ericsson, K. A. & Smith, J. (eds) *Towards a General Theory of Expertise* Cambridge: Cambridge University Press, 39–63.

Chase, W. G. & Simon, H. A. 1973 'Perception in chess'. *Cognitive Psychology* 4: 55–81

Chi, M. T. H., Feltovich, P. J. & Glaser, R. 1981 'Categorization and representation of physics problems by experts and novices'. *Cognitive Science* 5: 121–52.

Chi, M. T. H., Glaser, R. & Farr, M. J. (eds) 1988 *The Nature of Expertise* Hillsdale, NJ: Lawrence Erlbaum Associates.

Clark, C. M. & Yinger, R. J. 1979 *Three Studies of Teacher Planning* Research Series No. 55 East Lansing, Mich.: Institute for Research on Teaching, Michigan State University.

Clark, C. M. & Yinger, R. J. 1987 'Teacher planning'. In Calderhead, J. (ed.) *Exploring Teachers' Thinking* London: Cassell, 84–103.

Cohen, A. D. & Hosenfeld, C. 1981 'Some uses of mentalistic data in second language research'. *Language Learning* 31(2): 285–313.

Crookes, G. 1986 Task Classification: a Cross-disciplinary Review'. Center for Second Language Classroom Research, Social Science Research Institute, University of Hawaii.

De Groot, A. 1978 *Thought and Choice in Chess* The Hague: Mouton.

Ellis, G. & Sinclair, B. 1989 *Learning to Learn English* Cambridge: Cambridge University Press.

Ericsson, K. A. & Harris, M. 1989 'Acquiring expert memory performance without expert knowledge: a case study in the domain of chess'. Unpublished manuscript.

Ericsson, K. A. & Simon, H. A. 1978 'Retrospective verbal reports as data'. CIP Working Paper No. 388.

Ericsson, K. A. & Simon, H. A. 1980 'Verbal reports as data'. *Psychological Review* 87(3): 215–51.

Ericsson, K. A. & Simon, H. A. 1984 *Protocol Analysis: Verbal Reports as Data* Cambridge, Mass.: MIT Press.

Ericsson, K. A. & Simon, H. A. 1987 'Verbal reports on thinking'. In Færch, C. & Kasper, G. *Introspection in Second Language Research* Clevedon: Multilingual Matters, 24–53.

Ericsson, K. A. & Smith, J. 1991a (eds) *Towards a General Theory of Expertise* Cambridge: Cambridge University Press.

Ericsson, K. A. & Smith, J. 1991b 'Prospects and limits of the empirical study of expertise: an introduction'. In Ericsson, K. A. & Smith, J. (eds) *Towards a General Theory of Expertise* Cambridge: Cambridge University Press, 1–38.

Gilhooly, K. J. 1986 'Individual differences in thinking aloud performance'. *Current Psychological Research and Reviews* 5(4): 328–34.

Glaser, B. & Strauss, A. 1967 *Discovery of Grounded Theory* Chicago: Aldine.

Goh, C. 1998 'Strategic processing and metacognition in second language listening'. Unpublished PhD thesis, Lancaster University.

Green, A. 1998 *Verbal Protocol Analysis in Language Testing Research* Cambridge: University of Cambridge Local Examinations Syndicate, Cambridge University Press.

Haastrup, K. 1987 'Using thinking aloud and retrospection to uncover learners' lexical inferencing procedures'. In Færch, C. & Kasper, G. (eds) *Introspection in Second Language Research* Clevedon: Multilingual Matters, 197–212.

Halliday, M. A. K. 1970 'Language structure and language function'. In Lyons, J. (ed.) *New Horizons in Linguistics* Harmondsworth: Penguin.

Hayes, J. & Flower, L. 1983 'Uncovering cognitive processes in writing: an introduction to protocol analysis'. In Mosenthal, P. Tamor, L. & Walmsley, S. (eds) *Research in Writing: Principles and Methods* New York: Longman.

Hayes-Roth, B. & Hayes-Roth, F. 1979 'A cognitive model of planning'. *Cognitive Science* 3: 275–310.

Hunt, E. 1989 'Cognitive science: definition, status, and questions'. *Annual Review of Psychology* 40: 603–29.

Hutchinson, T. & Waters, A. 1987 *English for Specific Purposes* Cambridge: Cambridge University Press.

Irmscher, W. 1987 'Finding a comfortable identity'. *College Composition and Communication* February: 81–7.

Johnson, H. W. 1961 'Skills = speed × accuracy × form × adaptability'. *Perceptual and Motor Skills* 13: 163–70.

Johnson, K. 1996 *Language Teaching and Skill Learning* Oxford: Blackwell.

Johnson, K. 2000 'What task designers do'. *Language Teaching Research* 4(3): 301–21.

Johnson, K. 2001a *An Introduction to Foreign Language Learning and Teaching* London: Pearson Education (Longman).

Johnson, K. 2001b 'Is it a wood, or are they trees?' Paper delivered (as the Pit Corder Memorial Lecture) at the 2001 BAAL Annual Meeting. Mimeo.

Joseph, G. M. & Patel, V. J. 1986 'Specificity of expertise in clinical reasoning'. In *Program of the Eighth Annual Conference of the Cognitive Science Society* Hillsdale, NJ: Erlbaum, 331–45.

Kagan, D. 1988 'Teaching as clinical problem solving: a critical examination of the analogy and its implications'. *Review of Educational Research* 58: 482–505.

Krahnke, K. 1987 *Approaches to Syllabus Design for Foreign Language Teaching* Englewood, NJ: Prentice Hall.

Krutetskii, V. A. 1976 *The Psychology of Mathematical Problem Solving* Chicago: University of Chicago Press.

Kumaravadivelu, B. 1993 'The name of the task and the task of naming: methodological aspects of task-based methodology'. In Crookes, G. & Gass, S. M. *Tasks in a Pedagogical Context* Clevedon: Multilingual Matters, 69–96.

Lampert, M. D. & Ervin-Tripp, S. M. 1993 'Structured coding for the study of language and social interaction'. In Edwards, J. A. & Lampert, M. D. (eds) *Talking Data: Transcription and Coding in Discourse Research* Hillsdale, NJ: Lawrence Erlbaum Associates, 169–206.

Legge, D. and Barber, P. J. 1976 *Information and Skill* London: Methuen.

Lofland, J. (1971) *Analyzing Social Settings: a Guide to Qualitative Observation and Analysis* Belmont, Calif.: Wadsworth.

Long, M. 1985 'A role for instruction in second language acquisition: task-based language training'. In Hyltenstam, K. & Pienemann, M. (eds) *Modelling and Assessing Second Language Acquisition* Clevedon: Multilingual Matters, 77–100.

McDonough, J. 1998 'Learner training'. In Johnson, K. and Johnson, H. (eds) *Encyclopedic Dictionary of Applied Linguistics* Oxford: Blackwell Publishers, 193–5.

Miles, M. B. & Huberman, A. M. 1994 *Qualitative Data Analysis* 2nd edn. London: Sage.

Minsky, M. & Papert, S. 1974 *Artificial Intelligence* Condensed lectures, Oregon State System of Higher Education, Eugene.

Murray, D. 1983 'Response of a laboratory rat – or, being protocoled'. *College Composition and Communication* 34(2): 169–72.

Naiman, N., Fröhlich, H., Stern, H. & Todesco, A. 1978 *The Good Language Learner* Ontario Institute for Studies in Education: Research in Education Series, 7.

Newell, A. & Simon, H. A. 1972 *Human Problem Solving* Englewood Cliffs, NJ: Prentice-Hall.

Nunan, D. 1989 *Designing Tasks for the Communicative Classroom* Cambridge: Cambridge University Press.

Ormerod, T. C., Fritz, C. O. & Ridgway, J. 1999 'From deep to superficial categorisation with increasing expertise'. Paper delivered at 21st Annual Conference of the Cognitive Science Society, Vancouver, BC, Canada, August.

Oxford, R. 1990 *Language Learning Strategies: What Every Teacher Should Know* Rowley, Mass.: Newbury House.

Patel, V. L. & Groen, G. J. 1991 'The general and specific nature of medical expertise: a critical look'. In Ericsson, K. A. & Smith, J. (eds) *Towards a General Theory of Expertise* Cambridge: Cambridge University Press, 93–125.

Perez, R. S., Fleming Johnson, J. & Emery, C. D. (1995) 'Instructional design expertise: a cognitive model of design'. *Instructional Science* 23: 321–49.

Peterson, P. L., Marx, R. W. & Clark, C. M. 1978 'Teacher planning, teacher behaviour and student achievement'. *American Educational Research Journal* 15(3): 417–32.

Pólya, G. 1945 *How to Solve it* Princeton: Princeton University Press.

Prabhu, N. S. 1987 *Second Language Pedagogy: a Perspective* Oxford: Oxford University Press.

Reitman, W. 1965 *Cognition and Thought* New York: Wiley.

Samuda, V., Johnson, K. & Ridgway, J. 2000 *Designing Language Learning Tasks: a Guide* Vol. 1 *Draft* Working Papers on Task Design 1, Department of Linguistics and Modern English Language, University of Lancaster.

Scardamalia, M. & Bereiter, C. 1991 'Literate expertise'. In Ericsson, K. A. & Smith, J. (eds) *Towards a General Theory of Expertise* Cambridge: Cambridge University Press, 172–94.

Schoenfeld, A. H. 1985 *Mathematical Problem Solving* Orlando: Academic Press.

Shavelson, R. J. & Stern, P. 1981 'Research on teachers' pedagogical thoughts, judgments, decisions, and behaviour'. *Review of Educational Research* 51(4): 455–98.

Simon, H. A. 1981 *The Sciences of the Artificial* Cambridge, Mass.: MIT Press.

Sinclair, J. and Coulthard, M. 1975 *Towards an Analysis of Discourse* Oxford: Oxford University Press.

Skehan, P. 1998 *A Cognitive Approach to Language Learning* Oxford: Oxford University Press.

Smagorinsky, P. 1989 'The reliability and validity of protocol analysis'. *Written Communication* 6(4): 463–79.

Stratton, P. & Hayes, N. 1988 *A Student's Dictionary of Psychology* London: Edward Arnold.

Strauss, A. 1987 *Qualitative Analysis for Social Scientists* Cambridge: Cambridge University Press.

Strauss, A. & Corbin, J. 1990 *Basics of Qualitative Research* 1st edn. Thousand Oaks, Calif.: Sage.

Strauss, A. & Corbin, J. 1998 *Basics of Qualitative Research* 2nd edn. Thousand Oaks, Calif.: Sage.

Sutton, R. I. 1987 'The process of organizational death: disbanding and reconnecting'. *Administrative Science Quarterly* 32: 570–89.

Swales, J. M. 1990 *Genre Analysis: English in Academic and Research Settings* Cambridge: Cambridge University Press.

Taylor, P. H. 1970 *How Teachers Plan their Courses* Slough: National Foundation for Educational Research.

Tomlinson, B. (ed.) 1998 *Materials Development in Language Teaching* Cambridge: Cambridge University Press.

Tyler, R. W. 1950 *Basic Principles of Curriculum and Instruction* Chicago: Chicago University Press.

Voss, J. F., Green, T. R., Post, T. A. & Penner, B. C. 1983 'Problem solving skill in the social sciences'. In Bower, G. (ed.) *The Psychology of Learning and Motivation* Vol. 17. New York: Academic Press.

Wilkins, D. A. 1972 'Grammatical, situational and notional syllabuses'. Reprinted in Brumfit, C. J. & Johnson, K. (eds) *The Communicative Approach to Language Teaching* Oxford: Oxford University Press, 1979: 82–90.

Willis, J. 1996 *A Framework for Task-based Learning* London: Longman.

Woods, D. 1996 *Teacher Cognition in Language Teaching: Beliefs, Decision-making and Classroom Practice* Cambridge: Cambridge University Press.

Wright, T. 1987 'Instructional task and discoursal outcome in the L2 classroom'. In Candlin, C. N. & Murphy, D. F. (eds) *Language Learning Tasks* London: Prentice Hall, 47–68.

Yinger, R. J. 1977 'A study of teacher planning: description and theory development using ethnographic and information processing methods'. Unpublished doctoral dissertation, Michigan State University.

Zahorik, J. A. 1975 'Teachers' planning models'. *Educational Leadership* 33: 134–9

Index